88

A Journal Of Contemporary
American Poetry

Issue 2 - October 2002

Hollyridge Press
Venice, California

Managing Editor
Ian Randall Wilson

Hollyridge Press
P.O. Box 2872
Venice, California 90294

Cover Design by D.L. Stevens

Manufactured in the United States of America by Lightning Source

ISBN: 0-9676003-6-7

Indexed by: The American Humanities Index; The Index of American
Periodical Verse; Poem Finder on the Web; MLA Bibliography and MLA
Directory of Periodicals.

88: A Journal of Contemporary American Poetry is published annually by
Hollyridge Press. Please see the last pages of the issue for specific submission
information. Copyright reverts to authors on publication though in the event
of a reprint we ask for courtesy credit.

88's naming is something of a mystery. Some say it was named in homage
to Alfred Stieglitz's *291*. Others suggest that the numerals are taken from
the address of the editor's late relatives. Still another version is that the
upright double-infinity signs suggest boundless imagination. It just may be
that the anapest sounds good to the ear, feels good to the mouth.

Hollyridge Press is a small press publisher located in Venice, California. Using
Print-On-Demand technology, Hollyridge Press, publishes primarily literary
fiction. Print-On-Demand allows Hollyridge Press to maintain modest overhead
through low initial print costs and minimal inventory. Books are always in print
and available through wholesalers Ingram and Baker & Taylor.

Contents

Editor's Note to the Second Issue

Ronald Alexander
The Conservatory... 1

William Allegrezza
[father. . .] 2
[the light in the hall . . .]... 3

Barry Ballard
Blisters 4

Jim Barnes
Always Completely at Home 5

Aaron Belz
In Verity... 6

Bill Berkson
Thuringian Equals.. 7

Rick Bursky
When My Father Broke A Window 8

Justin Israel Cain
Lost Arts 9

Killarney Clary
[One, at least . . .].. 11

Cathy Colman
Letter To Well-Being From Babylon.. 12
I Lied About The Suicide Question: Letter To Fear 13

Patricia Corbus
She Stares Into Space... 14

Stephen Corey
Abjuring Political Poetry 15
Strengthening the Myth.. 16

Catherine Daly
Review: *Dying for Beauty* by Gail Wronsky.............................. 17

Stuart Dischell
Half Himself... 21

Patrick Donnelly
To A Variegated Begonia 24
Invitation To Ms. Martha Rhodes.. 26

Mark DuCharme
    Duplicate Hurries 29
kari edwards
    original color contrast 33
Kate Fetherston
    Lessons with the Devil 34
Zack Finch
    Scaffolding 36
Kevin S. Fitzgerald
    Revenant 37
    A Ruse is a Ruse is a Ruse 38
Chris Forhan
    Essay: When I Say 'I': Poets' Use Of The First Person 39
Richard P. Gabriel
    Essence of Memory 58
    Lesson 59
Richard Garcia
    Hollywood 60
    Not Bad for a Hermaphrodite 61
J.F. Garmon
    Autumn Drunk 63
Eric Gelsinger
    Steam or, Luck 64
Reginald Gibbons
    Summer 65
Joy Gladding
    Sprouting Grass Moon 66
Elton Glaser
    Damage Control 67
Rachel Hadas
    The Nap and the Gentleman Caller 69
Shauna Hannibal
    An Annunciation 70
    Stay, ... 71
Matt Hart
    Scary Rowboat 72
    At the Moment I Am Unwilling 73
    Review: *Tremolo* by Spencer Short 75

Terrance Hayes
    Mausoleum.. 78
    Seabrooks... 79
Dianna Henning
    Dust... 81
David Hess
    Whirled 82
George Higgins
    Mingus 83
Jonathan Holden
    Transitivity... 84
Roy Jacobstein
    Moths 86
Mark Jarman
    At the Broadway Exit... 87
Halvard Johnson
    Variations in C.. 88
    Alleged Variations 89
Kate Knapp Johnson
    The Meaning of Simplicity 91
Peter Johnson
    The Deep Footprints of God 93
Jeffrey Jullich
    mild aches: aware better path...................................... 94
    paying in full for services.. 96
Carolyn Lei-lanilau
    Xiandai: Modernity.. 97
Gerald Locklin
    at *the score* 98
Fred Moramarco
    My Shoes 99
Matt Morris
    Being & Being Dead... 100
Elisabeth Murawski
    Arms 103
Muriel Nelson
    Telltale 105

B.Z. Niditch
    A Frank O'Hara Day.. 106
Louis Phillips
    Johnny Inkslinger Presumes. 107
Lee Rossi
    Survivor 108
Mary Ruefle
    The Little I Saw of Cuba... 109
    Intermittence 110
Ravi Shankar
    Language Poetry 111
Ron Silliman
    --- 112
    Toward An Anniversary Of A Drowning In The Senses............ 115
    Storming Waumbec Mountain By Golf Cart............................. 116
Rick Smith
    From the Wren Notebook 117
Alan Sondheim
    The Continuity Girl... 118
    Take of the Continuity Girl.. 119
    Unit Mo... 120
    Biograph Continuity Girl 122
Denise L. Stevens
    September Catalogue 124
    f-stop 125
Terese Svoboda
    Nipple 127
Paula Szuchman
    The Terms... 128
James Tate
    Elegy For Spooky 129
    Jules to the Rescue 130
    Doppelganger.. 131
Judith Taylor
    Court Jester 132
Elaine Terranova
    Mint 134

Leslie Ullman
      The Other Life 135
Charles Harper Webb
      The Secret of Wyatt Earp... 137
Susan Wheeler
      Wait! 138
Eve Wood
      Hunter Green.. 139
Renate Wood
      Purgatory, Etc. 140
Gail Wronsky
      My Childhood, if it had Taken Place in an Actual Desert.......... 142
      Elegy from a Nightingale's Point of View 143

Contributors
Guidelines

EDITOR'S NOTE TO THE SECOND ISSUE

Sometimes the most apparent is the least obvious. One of our first contributors posited that *88* was named after a piano keyboard; we chose many different kinds of poetry which still made up a whole. I'll admit, only this once, that I had never thought of that explanation but claim it now. Several more exotic reasons are mentioned on the fly-leaf. I invite you to come up with others (for all of which I will then take credit).

88 has come into being because we've been able to take advantage of a relatively new technology: Print-on-Demand. The journal is created like any other book using desktop publishing software and then held in the memory of a printing machine somewhere in Tennessee. The machine can print a 300-page bound softcover book with a four-color cover in one minute. Our set-up costs are small and there's no requirement to print several thousand off-set copies which might sit in a closet somewhere for a long time. (Has everyone who's ever worked on a journal had this happen?) We only print copies for our contributors and a number of indexing services and reviewers. The rest of the work is done by the printer. An order as small as one book from Amazon or any good independent bookstore anywhere in the United States or a library comes in to wholesaler Ingram or Baker & Taylor then is sent on to the printer where it is fulfilled quickly. The finished book is sent to the bookstore and on to the reader. On Demand publishing makes it possible to keep *88* always in print and always available.

That's the technical side of things but what of philosophy and purpose? I've been reading Clayton Eshleman's new collection of essays (*Companion Spider*) and came across his introduction to the final issue of *Sulfur*. He said that after 20 years of publication he'd fulfilled his original mission. What is *88*'s mission? I wanted to enter into the literary dialogue that goes on in this country beneath the popular culture. I wanted to stop complaining about the work I read in other journals and make my own selection of what to publish. That way, good or bad (good I think so far), it would be my responsibility (or fault). In addition to the lyric and lyric-narrative poetry that seems to make up the mainstream these days, I also wanted to publish work that

I wasn't seeing in a number of other journals. I wanted to wear a green eye-shade and stay up past midnight pasting pages. I wanted to die with "rosebud" on my lips. I wanted to play God.

Already, between the first and second issues, there have been changes: Denise Stevens stepped down in order to devote more time to her own poetry, and I have assumed the mantle of managing editor. She continues to contribute her marvelous aesthetic to the selection process, and designed the cover again (with a bit of encouragement).

What does it mean to run a literary journal in 2002? I can tell you a lot of people want to be published. I'd love for someone in an essay to address the issue of what drives this need for publication. Some have complained that it's wrong to insist on a proof-of-purchase submission policy but we take our lead from other journals, notably *The Hudson Review*. I contend that poets have to support the journals they submit to. (And there is an open period when no such proof is required.)

Putting this journal together is a lot of work. When I read other editors' notes about the satisfaction they experienced from reading and then publishing a great poem, I wasn't sure I believed them. But so far it's actually true: You read and you know the poem is right. You know the poem is working. You know someone else needs to know it, too.

—Ian Randall Wilson, Los Angeles, October 2002

Ronald Alexander

THE CONSERVATORY

Dieffenbachia, ficus, schefflera, dracaena marginata: infinite variations of green. We exhaust our minds, matching mottled leaves and slotted shapes with botanical names on lettered plaques, spiked into the ground at the base of each plant. I take a breath of the musky air. We're alone in glass and iron: it's Sunday morning in the Conservatory. The suspended sprinklers yield unexpected drops of water; some splash our arms and faces; others roll across the surfaces and off the tips of tropical spears, fanned overhead in a jungle canopy. We round a corner, enter a new wing, and see an elderly couple just ahead; they've stopped and are stooped over the soil. The man steadies himself with his cane and turns to the woman to speak; he twists at the waist as if his corroded spine prohibits his head and neck from moving independent of his torso, and as we approach the woman cants her head and attempts a smile, but only the right corner of her mouth moves. The man touches the brim of his hat; his skin is pink as if it has been scrubbed too hard with a stiff-bristled brush and there are red splotches on his cheeks. He twists again to probe the ground with his cane, and then offers his arm to the woman but it's obvious that she is the one who is helping him. The synthetic sheen of his maroon shirt drapes his body shamelessly, and his checked trousers, I imagine, cover bruised and atrophied legs. They disappear around a leafy corner, and we step into their place to look at fragile, speckled orchids. Beyond the square, glass panes, lies Lincoln Park, its ground covered with frost, and there is nothing but bare, black earth to indicate where rows of vibrant, red cannas stretched to the fountain last summer. Inside this world without seasons, my lover looks ahead. When he twists and reaches out to me with an upturned palm, his movements are easy and spontaneous. The sun angles through the glass, filters through the fronds of a tall palm, and falls across his outstretched arm. I memorize the network of beryl veins on his biceps and forearm, certain now that the shelter of glass and iron cannot assuage the blue from fading. I step forward. He rests his hand on my shoulder and we walk on together without speaking.

William Allegrezza

[FATHER. . .]

father   the nothing of vision recedes
while tidal motions rearrange the slight curve of land
that retains the finding that no other answer remains but violence

"But mister"
       "The temple head preaches prosperity and inevitable
        mortality, and so I say, with
Alcaeus, drink to gods for light is short."

in evit   or ex it astoysleftrustingintheyard
for th en re a son cou ld com plain or at lea   st com ply
but no w onl   y bog monsters and fe ar

the number is long

William Allegrezza

[THE LIGHT IN THE HALL . . .]

the light in the hall
      shifts downwards
as beetles struggle or spiders find

      in motion is the morning
          and ships at sea

the answer for purgation remains purgation
      while vision is release through stages of forgetting
              but we've forgotten and forget

the broken climb   in late spring
      when children leave and the doors swing

the models are destruction

Barry Ballard

BLISTERS

This is my father's funeral, but it
isn't death. Death was days ago until
someone carried it away. (They distill
it into something we can drink, with a twist
of concealment to spare us or numb us.)
I look for horror in this place, for the screams
because nothing is at rest in the belief
of a soul separated from its own dust.

Instead, I believe my own hands blistered
and that I dug my father's grave, that I
wrapped his cold body in his own blanket,
struggling with its weight, condemned to carry
it in my aching arms, standing below
the scarred earth in its deep, crying shadow.

Jim Barnes

ALWAYS COMPLETELY AT HOME

The days we meant to stop in St. Maximin were
always full of sun and the lure of mountains toward
the north. We never did in all the passing of
the cloister take the time to find the narrow road
up to the door: we were not penitent enough
to drag our indolent bodies through the summer

heat that hung about us in haloes of blue flowers
from the Cézanne fields. Perhaps we were a bit afraid
of the spirits that we thought might still linger there
in the dark and gilted skull. Heaviness of monks made
us skirt holy ground and drive round the city square
where old men smoked and played boules in the slower hours

of Provençal afternoons. In all that passing,
we never stopped. And now, months past, our minds unfurl
that world: we are driving still in place: the steeple
of St. Maximin comes in view, and we see swirling
robes of prostitutes and pizza vans and a deep
dust rising from round a game of boules that will last

well into the evening hours. Still we drive on through
the broad fields and up the winding road past Pourrières
as we did before, waving at the old shepherd
with his fall flock near le Puits-d'Auzon, and the bare
summit of Ste. Victoire glows in the last light poured
from the sun, blessing all the valleys in rose and blue.

In the village that is Vauvenargues, we may atone
with an Amaretto—for we are lovers, wine
if we were not—and contemplate the azure valley
below our table or the château that is vined
with the tangled years of Picasso's art and folly.
He is, locals say, always completely at home.

Aaron Belz

IN VERITY

Salutations from St. Louis. The rain
has rained its white voice all day
while certain words have turned red
in my mind, certain phrases—"ants
in the cupboard," say, and "heresy."

Even so, honey retains its biting tang
and watered-down daylight pours
into a bay window in the drawing room.
So like a farmer I write and write,
casting down seed upon seed, resting

only while the dot matrix printer sings.
The song effects a drowsiness in me,
so I descend into the patterns and objects
of letters: "Dear Adrian, we miss you;
come soon; the aphids are blooming,

though the violets have roses. Honeycup,
I love you like a soft-bodied insect, I
love you in the smell of sluggy grass,
with the distance of a swingset. There is
a rotten hammer underneath the deck,

and on the wicker table a bright glass." We
nap beneath the blue spring sun, turtle-like,
while words play musical chairs in our heads;
through the screen I see a copper basket
full of limes and pears, apples and candies.

Bill Berkson

THURINGIAN EQUALS

A book where everybody, reader and writer included, dies.

The kind of thing people said in the 1970s: "Hello, I'm back being me again."

My first and last names and the first and last names of both my parents have the same number of letters.

A distant yet achingly distinct whinny: *et voila!* the walking buckboard.

Dustin Hoffman's bookcase hanging by one hinge out onto Eleventh Street, dawn 1969.

Telephone solicitation for a ballet school in need of "serious floorboards."

The thought of someone flat on his back on the carpet, tossing and giggling.

For the second time in two millennia slept through the meteor shower, results of last night's talk.

Rick Bursky

WHEN MY FATHER BROKE A WINDOW

My mother saved him from seven years
bad luck by putting it back together.
Weeks of sitting on the floor
with tweezers, magnifier and glue.
The finished glass had hundreds of lines
that made us appear older.
We took turns staring at ourselves.
Everyone ages, my mother said.
One piece of glass was never found.
When you looked in the mirror
it seemed that there was hole in your face
the shape of an island on a pirate's map.
Then my father disappeared.

My mother said he climbed in the hole
searching for whatever hid at the bottom of the dark
and we wouldn't see him for seven years.
Each evening she put his dinner in the hole.
When we were evicted she wrote
our new address on a scrap of paper
and taped it to the mirror.
By the time he returned
the paper and his skin had turned brown.

Justin Israel Cain

LOST ARTS

When it's more likely someone said,
I'll stay on this planet and rest awhile
still in hordes we wonder, in heaps regret.
Serendipity is a funny word, but gallimaufry
really cracks me up. The Narwhal is an Arctic
sea animal related to the Dolphin.
There's always something left to play with.
So much for opening remarks. Let's talk Femtoseconds.
More are in one second than total seconds
in the last 31 million years.
This makes it impossible to catch up with
dirty laundry or Gibbon's book on the Roman Empire,
of which I'm stuck on page two.
I can't get past how a tropical climate
repelled the invading Legion
back to their cruise ship with Captain Mars.
I think they would've enjoyed the weather.
The outer worlds are named after fallen gods.
Good for them, but what does this say about
our need for aesthetic distance throughout the universe?
Is there any hope? Does anyone care?
Of course we do, though my composition class won't admit it.
Half dropped out when I said,
write as if you're conversing with someone you love.
Stats for the semester: 62% slept through
the attack of dangling modifiers while 38%
transmorphed into an amorously famished umbrage of cuckoo.
The teacher can be infinitely reduced.
Soon to be revealed: why we've been called here.
Heading this way: a collapsible galaxy
colonized by 80 foot sheep.
If Nancy applies the Theory of Relativity

on her trip to Denver, a distance of 70 miles,
how much will she age?
Upon her return, will she recognize me?
Probably not. I'm changing again and don't know what to do.
A Magpie might have the answer, but it's not talking.
Ditto: the mountain, corn stalk and coffee pot.
Though they provide some pleasure, if life is fleeting
I'd rather not dwell on what remains.
Shoes look awkward when lying in a pile,
but in the middle of an orgy, please remain calm.

Killarney Clary

[ONE, AT LEAST . . .]

One, at least, had come in advance, paced from town to town—
maybe to lay a map. A shadow arced then faded before a moonless
night. One whose boots crumbled the desert grit, who fidgeted with
his keys in his pocket because he had finished his task and was
standing, cooling in the dark, listening. "Include this," he laughed to
himself. "Arrange in your plan the measureless things—the sense,
even now, in the pitch, of something passing above, how it makes
me flinch and shy, raise my arm."

Cathy Colman

LETTER TO WELL-BEING FROM BABYLON

All this time I was leading the life of the healthy,
of loam and the limbo that mimics pleasure,
like the white spaces in Cézanne, the "diamond zones
of God" he left on purpose because colors were all he knew
for certain. White fields of harvest.
As time dreams itself into being
and then wakes up and remembers it's already
been done.

As once I had to have sex immediately
after lunch under the pergola and then came the talk
about Babylon and Presence,
and all those minutes I was living another life, opening
and shutting drawers from which I plucked
this or that metal or sequined eye-gleam. I was champion
of folding towels and that gaze, out, out into the yellow room
of outdoors, the mountains with their muscled backs
upon which I climbed, unafraid.

This is where I must look for you, now, my
other, my resemblance, find you with no map, no twin compasses
of Donne. You know how this is:
it's not just the pain itself—it's the pain of the pain, skin of my skin.
Grief is female.
Eating the bloody sack and the whole
child, if she must, in order, somehow,
to save it.

Cathy Colman

I LIED ABOUT THE SUICIDE QUESTION: LETTER TO FEAR

For no good reason, the afterlife seemed appealing, though empty
of meat thought.
And true friends. Haven't I also, at times, been a betrayer?
Baffled myself in the newly reconciled couples' mirror
over the mantelpiece, the one that always reflected a little too much
of the bamboo of paradise.
There was a twilight on the patio that had been rehearsed.
I felt the ripe fear that comes for no good reason or for a good
one, like the evening we looked in the sky and saw a shimmering
UFO signature.

Some day I'll know the unraveling of the fleshly engines.
The dismantling, surge and expiation. Body against body until
the pigment changes, the last scintilla of sex.
Yours was pink like a baby that had been preserved or plucked
clean each night.
I craved it because I was craved by it.
Like a dip in the Ganges, blessed and forever tainted.

For no good reason, I'm still involved with the business of fear.
Not just of death. But the longing to rid myself of the self.
Where the fear lives. Mutant but somehow welcome.
Be humble before it, something said.
Or does it have its own bass voice?
Its own real pearl earrings?

Patricia Corbus

SHE STARES INTO SPACE

Sometimes a storm breaks through a window
and moves in, but things rarely happen here:

a shoebox eclipse now and then, various
Cavaliers and Puritans, vainglorious victims

and aggressors in dirt alleyways, heads stuffed
in dustbuckets, the fading sound of birdsong.

—But there, the vast loneliness of fledgling
planets, bitter-smelling rocks in empty rivers,

not decaying in patience like houses or bodies
slowly sinking—but firming, moons jockeying

like China juggled out of a cupboard, sills
of valleys leaning over, learning mold and lichen.

The loneliness of these child planets!—their
gargantuan dusks, unthinking applegreen sunsets,

not one sparrow in a tree, not one martyr
or lover crying for a lost mate, brooded over,

brooding. Garnet-green pools engulf smaller pools
without quenching one thirst—yet all things

breathe in and out. Clouds pump their wings
and erupt into geysers, constellations sway,

collapse and smash like chandeliers. The debris
became fish, then mermaids, then girls—*then me.*

Stephen Corey

ABJURING POLITICAL POETRY

Some men will shoot an infant in the face.
There, that's a start—near pentameter, even.
Has the world been bettered yet, or your mood?

The only mirror of horror is itself.
Art's a game when it thinks it shows the world
in actuality; art's a savior
when it stalks the world as art: stone as stone,
paint as paint, words as the music of words.

Here's a joke we children laughed at once:
*What's the difference between a truckload
of bowling balls and one of dead babies?
You can't unload the balls with a pitchfork.*

It's okay to laugh—that shows you sense the awfulness.
Imagine the hearer who did not get the joke:
No poem could reach him. No horror. No world.

Stephen Corey

STRENGTHENING THE MYTH

Really, Medusa's the easy way out,
those snakes for hair a weak side glance
at what needed seeing. Hair is merely decorative,
merely dead. Let's have snakes from the throat
roiling out over the lips, or snakes from the anus,
or maybe one snake from each eye.

My grandpa, one hundred and one, shuffles
the small green corridor, catheter
trailing—they're wed now forever, these two.
Tendons still course his body, but with power
no longer their name, nor tautness their gift.

Dear god, we should say, make us rock.
Cast not upon us again thine eye
that lets us go soft, lets us rot.

Catherine Daly

REVIEW:
DYING FOR BEAUTY by GAIL WRONSKY
Copper Canyon, 2000. $14.00

Gail Wronsky's *Dying for Beauty* represents a decade of poetic development from the neo-surreal poems and series poems in her first book, *Again the Gemini are in the Orchard* (named after a painting by Leonora Carrington, that book's informing intelligence). *Dying for Beauty* demonstrates Wronsky's facility in the sort of contemporary lyrical long poem which seems to be eluding serious critical attention. A generation of female poets is writing the long poem at an unprecedented level of poetic power. Graham, Swensen, Notley, and Blau DuPlessis have recently published long poems, serial poems, poetic sequences, and extended projects in poetry. In "Earth as Desdemona," working from a relationship of mother nature to mother tongue, Wronsky reassigns Othello as humankind and Desdemona as the earth, and then updates their familiar story. In "Sor Juana's Last Dream," she writes Sor Juana into wisdom poetry.

In this book, Wronsky's earlier taut and compact but light and fragile phrasing is replaced by writing not nearly as honed, but more dramatic, and with a fuller tone. The risk with economical phrasing is flatness. The dialogic qualities of "Earth as Desdemona" make Wronsky's address more direct, and increase the range of its interpretability. For example, when Wronsky writes

> Look, here's an emptiness, he said.
>
> An emptiness of earthworms, even of
> shellfish and of sponges. . .
>
> Death.
>
> No, that is not it. That is still not it.
>
> You. Come closer. . .   (21)

"you" is made parallel to "death," and the direct address, to the reader, the earth, and Desdemona, is menacing, but slowly and quietly menacing, menacing in a colloquial way. In the conversation, the male portion is simpler than the drifting, "of earthworms, even of shellfish and sponges" followed by an ellipsis, as though the female speaker could babble on, listing simple creatures of the earth and sea. When the female portion continues "No, that is not it. That is still not it." the repetition demonstrates the speaker is unsuccessful at negating death and unsuccessful at convincing the male portion of anything. However, still on the page, the female speaker's negation of the negative equation of emptiness, death, and the womb would indicate a positive equation of the womb, life, and fecund nature. This is how the poem continues, with the speaker now the writer and identified with the earth and Desdemona:

> I was leisurely everywhere: a woman
> self-possessed, a fat girl loving her own gravel
> laughter . . .
> . . .
>
> I shouted, *Bridegrooms, come quick!*
> *Come romp around my rind!*
> *I am gentle, Egyptian, and divine! Clasp me,*
> *delicatest machine!*   (22)

The risk of neo-surrealism is that meanings are obscure or unintended, and the poetry's claim of complexity doesn't seem justified. Here, the meanings are deliberately and carefully constructed, and the more generous language makes them more colloquial and readable.

Aside from Othello and Desdemona, other characters in *Dying for Beauty* are also familiar from earlier poetry and theater. Sor Juana and Walt Whitman join characters from Egyptian, Greek, and Aztec mythology. "Tonight, Walt Whitman, The Pacific" is not truly Whitmanesque. The poem invites and includes Whitman with its repetition of the phrases "let's celebrate" and "we'll celebrate." The poem is important to the book because it is an intertextual occasional poem written for Ted Danson's American Oceans Campaign. This particular organization is the one which informs Wronsky's environmentalism, and therefore the environmentalism in her poems. For example, the poem mentions celebrating the *absence* of oil drilling in certain parts of the California coastline. The American Oceans Campaign led to the foundation of Environmental Problem Solving, which in turn helped Copper Canyon fund publication of this book. Copper Canyon Press has always supported environmental causes.

Sor Juana's "Primero Sueño" is an epistemological poem, a study or a theory of the nature and grounds of knowledge. Unlike many of Sor Juana's other poems and plays, "Primero Sueño" was written in the style of Luis de Gongora. Gongorism is a highly decorated baroque style full of latinisms which is also proto-surrealist. The style can inform a reading of the work of surrealist poets Philip Lamantia and Will Alexander. Sor Juana's poem uses bizarre symbols and hermetic shapes such as obelisks, as does Wronsky's poem "Sor Juana's Last Dream." Stylistically, Wronsky's poem more closely resembles a particularly famous translation of "Primero Sueño": that of Samuel Beckett, hired by Octavio Paz for his Mexican poetry anthology. Beckett's translation of the preface of "Primero Sueño" simplifies the meanings, and makes no attempt to indicate the over-the-top style of the original or the original's inspiration. Wronsky's poem is written toward her strengths, which include command of a wide subject matter and dramatic setting.

The Wronsky poem encompasses the most striking elements of the original: its status as a wisdom poetry, its references to wisdom poetry of the Incas and Maya, and its inclusion of the "exotic." Wisdom poetry was correctly identified by Sor Juana and here by Wronsky as one of the sources of long poetry in general and non-epic long poetry in particular. While the Hebrew Bible, especially Proverbs, contains one type of wisdom poetry, so many long ancient poems which are not epics are wisdom poetry: Hesiod's "Theogeny," ancient Egyptian texts including Ptahhotep's "Maxims," and the Anglo-Saxon "Dream of the Rood." Wronsky's poem is focused on the way the beauty of Sor Juana's poetry first led to the death of her permission to write ("Our God / eats women," 80) and finally lead to her own death:

> I'll leave you my bundle:
>
> my nightmare:
> . . .
>
> It's a pyramid no one will
> translate effectively—
> the ink black glaze of a poet
>
> made palpable. It's everything
> but
> what's been said.   (88)

Contemporary readers of ambitious and new poetry continue to look beyond mythopoetics for a feminist long poetry which conquers giant, important subjects like life, history, and religion. They will find what they look for in Wronsky's fine second book.

Stuart Dischell

HALF HIMSELF

I

In sunlight beside a dry November pool,
The vinyl slatted outdoor furniture
Left impressions in the pastel linen
Of his out of season suit. From his perch
He appraised the tiled roofs and the wakes
Of container vessels ploughing the sea
Beyond the harbor. Was it really November?
The morning heat undignified as an August
Noon, little pearls of coffee sweat clung
To the lip of his cup. Last night a kiss,
Her tongue like a duchess in salon among
The collected statuary, went no further.
His vow was old as the knights he drew
On napkins and memoranda. Another face
Had been his grail. He had had his chance,
The choosing done, questions poorly answered.
His heart was an empty bed; his body
The sole hotel guest. His room was waiting
Above the veranda, its window affording
The bellman and maid the fine view of him.

II

But who was he to be seen as such,
A so-and-so no longer up and up,
Exile to the inappropriate month,
His topcoat on the chairback hung
Like the director's of another era
Of wide lapels and the teeming pool
And the band playing a foreign strain

For the Bacchus of the course
And the willows in their shorts
Sipping brightly colored drinks
In the closing fire of the sun;
Time for the credits in the large font
To see who played whom and never skip
Those happy names that spring to health
From the deepest lake or vein-fed well
A fountain to the arid land,
Otherwise an insubstantial self,
The image of a character of film
Projected in the out of doors
Over brickwork and molding.

III

Someone's air force is leaving
Vapor trails in the cerulean sky,
And someone's enterprise is hauling
Letters above the shoreline,
Avowals of love in bold caps,
Mile high promotions for local
Eating and drinking establishments.
Goodbye to the world of slow recognition.
Hello to the news of the too-close plane,
A reminder of the industrial machinery
That is always grinding somewhere,
Like the drone of a distant lecture
When he was a student of someone,
And the body of knowledge was near
As a classmate guiding his hands.
Something was imminent then,
Like a figure stepping out of its clothes,
Like a figure climbing out of the pool
Rung by rung up the steel ladder.

IV

He wrote a letter on the hotel stationary,
Its salutation in a clear, broad hand.
The *dear* seemed intimate though forced.
Already he detected the problem of tone.
Folding it over he wanted it right
Like the cleft in a windsor knot.
The water's solution proved reflective.
He prefaced the *dear* with *my*,
Attaining a little of the personal
Yet brusque in his mannered way,
This peculiar state he was heir to,
Monarch of transparency, born
To the confiscated lands, whose dear
Deposed heads acquired their fame
For squandering familial misfortune.
He would accept the generous offer
Of her car and driver. He would pay
The anticipated visit. The management
Had made all the necessary arrangements.
Comb, toothbrush, and razor in his pocket.

24 / Issue 2 — October 2002

Patrick Donnelly

TO A VARIEGATED BEGONIA

I stole a cutting of you, star-shaped leaves on blood-red stems,
from an old Jewish woman whose apartment I cleaned
twenty years ago when I was a starving actor,
and now that I am a starving poet
somehow you are still springing gamely from a new pot
which you have only inhabited since last July
when you and I moved into this house.
You have had a succession of pots, and plates
under your pots, just as I have had a succession
of rented apartments in which I have lived with you,
but somehow you and I have always managed
to have a garden with the kind of shade you like
in inexpensive Brooklyn in the summer.

This is your best incarnation—
finally on the *piano nobile* of an old brownstone
with plenty of light that wakes us both up about 7 A.M.,
your roots secure
in earthenware from Mexico I found on the street
that still smells strongly of someone else's rosemary.
All those years in the English basement
with its floods and mice and molds and neighbors
who seemed to stomp deliberately on the floor are over.

But I don't know if you are the same you
with whom I've lived for twenty years,
just as I'm not sure I am the same I
who carried a slip of you home on the subway in a jar
with a little wet paper towel, or the same I
who has often gone and left you
in a dish of water for weeks at a time,
telling you I hoped you would make it

but I can't live my life to suit a plant goddammit,
as I went out the door again and again
to investigate some boy in the Bronx,
in California, in Florida, in Amsterdam,
who wouldn't turn out to be the one.

Patrick Donnelly

INVITATION TO MS. MARTHA RHODES

October 11, 2001

To Brooklyn, over the Brooklyn Bridge, on this fine morning,
    please come flying.
Out of a cloud of fiery pale chemicals,
    please come flying,
to the tune of relief funds and financial packages
descending out of the mackerel sky,
over the panic of harbor-water,
    please come flying.

Smoke, multitudes of flags and spores are blowing. The ships
in the harbor are supposed to be ours, the pilots
for the moment just joking and chilling, and handsome policemen prying
into anything untoward. The flight is safe,
the guest room is arranged,
    please come flying.

Come with good Victorian jewelry discreetly flashing,
Manhattan is awash with mortality this fine morning,
At the Gate of the city barbarians are shaking
their fists while we crave their *Perfect Disappearance*.
When you plug in your phone at my place,
    it will already be ringing,
    please come flying.

For whom the urns on the Promenade are full to overflowing
with spiky palm, ageratum and geranium—
there are Four Ways of traveling:
(mounting the sky with natural heroism,
above the accidents, above the malignant movies)
by bridge, ferry, blimp, or swimming—
    but please come flying.

We can sit down and weep; we can go shopping,
or we can bravely deplore, but please
    please come flying.
With dynasties of negative constructions
darkening and dying around you,
come for a week, a month, come
until the mayor's divorce is final,
to the Brooklyn Academy of Music where Whitman is still waiting
for Caruso and Galli-Curci to stop their trilling—
Maria Anna Cecilia Sophia Meneghini Kalogeropoulos Callas
was supposed to be singing, but since she died she's always canceling—
    but anyway
    please come flying.

The little ocher dredge off the end of your dock is working
to make the Hudson deeper,
filling huge gray barges around the clock—
dump cat food on the floor, come
away from the buildings stove in like torn-open, unanswered letters,
and not yet salvaged, if they ever will be—
forget the shower, delay the laundry,
out of all that untidy activity
awful and not the least bit cheerful,
    please come crawling.

A call to the gardener at Brooklyn Botanic this precarious morning
couldn't confirm if *The Camperdown Elm* is dead or living—
it would be so helpful just now
    for it still to be lifting
    its mist of fine twigs.
And we are relying on that hollowness, which the Bartlett tree specialist
thrust his arm the whole length of, and the six small cavities also,
    all expectations defying.

At the end of every day the burning mound is shrinking,
the man with the tablecloth
isn't falling or dying;
actuarial tables have stopped drifting
onto the roof—whatever is still smoldering
isn't yet catching onto anything we love, so
come like that poem we've got by Hart
Crane, springing Ringling, Barnum and Bailey
over the fine long span by Roebling:
to Brooklyn, over the Brooklyn Bridge, on this fine morning,
    please come flying.

Mark DuCharme

DUPLICATE HURRIES

Down the window if they're missing:

Words
Standing in for (one
An-) other words (standing) patiently

As you read these lines, the house is
Catching fire

Convivial to
Market protection sunrise
Without the cuffs, or
Scoffs at duping

Idle experiment equals work (residue)

'Yuck, that is not what I confiscated'

Nasally, spastically

Constructs while slipping
The way the waves
Flicker
For now, sucker

Either lifelessly, or it runs out

A kind of idle action insert

In the inert, colored glass

Mottled as a kind of flame

For the conditionally under-recorded

The purity of the faucet
In its disinclination

Qua 'message'

But *is it* a saturation job?
That's one way to describe it
Actually, I'm not interested in describing it

Blue at an alarming rate
Though 'kittenish' (several others laugh)

Stem of Polynesian ink
Mica trembling through blue acoustics

My design for a new dollar bill
Sucks Jesus
This guy has a tape of it

In the morning the plazas were
Broken

Drafted, in its free-form rotation—

The original is temporarily
Unavailable

On a starry night, with so many fat tickets

Here is a How-To Riddle:

What major appliances
Went totally undreamt of
Before the war, in Italian gardens?

Confine your answers to one piece of paper
Loosely torn
Then stuck in the mouth

Here is one economics problem:

How many Euros does it take

(Held softly between
For the fruits are spoiled)—

Obsolescence as a course of slenderizing

I'm just asking you to be aware of it

Driven to impertinent spillage:

The manic

Rivers

Hinged

kari edwards

ORIGINAL COLOR CONTRAST

I couldn't remember re I couldn't remember rugs re that needed a . . .
I don't remember, I remember the night measure, a remade film, a
horse of a different that wasn't that couldn't be. I said I could measure
the measured—the rational irrational. I could measure a thimble on a
very large scale, larger than the earth's surface in a transcendental—I
could touch the lost horizon in a three quarter—here and there. I had
wanted squares and triangles. I could say—circles. real ones, I could
say—imaginary ones disturbed me. they were complex, they circled
in and couldn't be measured, they could or couldn't stand on their
own. I counted the edges that begged for the borders, imaginary borders
to measure in broader borders that lay in double piles. while I lay in
four color content, or an unmade bed, or necessities displaced.

Kate Fetherston

LESSONS WITH THE DEVIL

First he offers tea in a cinder
block room on an unmade bed.
A white carton of cigarettes careens
against the whiskey bottles on a shelf.
Through the open window summer voices
lull and buzz. I try to explain how I need
help with my poems when
I realize the devil isn't
listening. He interrupts, wanting to know if
I can see his aura—which I can but
it isn't shiny. The top of his head
just melts into blank block walls.
So, next he strokes his chin, confides,
To become a poet takes as long
as it takes water to discover water
and then to forgive itself.
I'm digesting this alchemy when
the devil, warming to my audience, warns
of certain tendencies toward the pure
that are premature and out of sync
in my work. Later, while we walk outside,
he fishes a corkscrew from his pocket,
flips it into the air, and gets to his real
point. *That man is not for you.*
Tell me you aren't with him. He's bad news.
I should know. The devil snaps
his fingers and the corkscrew flashes.
Pewter clouds eclipse the sun.
I am waiting for a brimstone
symphony, for night to bludgeon
my bruised heart, for him to say
something that will finish

me off. But light streaks back
out of glowering nimbus clouds
and the grass is green
again and he is just a man and we
go on walking like that.

Zack Finch

SCAFFOLDING

Let's say I'd been thinking frozen rivers, all day of jade,
Popping capsules for emotions. I'd been whistling through
The same bad teeth for months, looking like the gray

Newsprint of New Haven. Color led me astray.
The particulars elate or hurt.
Or my habits as thus envisaged are projections

Of the framework of the English sentence. In the room,
The paraplegic was practicing his typewriter. I
Miss you. From the center of my text. I can't stop

Stubbing cigarette butts into the melon rind. That is:
After six years in a grocery, in the middle of a tropical syntax,
She told me she'd been seeing someone else. I threw up

The bodhisattvah shield. Raw / emotion is repulsive to exchange.
What control! The motorcyclist's knee just brushed the ground!
Donatello's horseman in the blue spring dawn steps out into the dew.

This was typed. The pigments were whittled out of lazuli, proof
For the materiality of poems. All loss has this thingly character.
Stirring, the willows bend. The willows bend. They won't let go.

Kevin S. Fitzgerald

REVENANT

Chalk groves of cypress in ghost walks buffeted by shallows
or shadows, by shade or umbra. Nude or nothing and null
transports whispering among rain on all souls hollow.
Arpeggios blanched the surface with inwardness among
ascetic nights of the return to the return.

Kevin S. Fitzgerald

A RUSE IS A RUSE IS A RUSE

He remained glacial among the floes in Grand Central and descended into the throes, the thick of it brandishing a disposable umbrella. Skimming the corrugated surface, he hummed some deplorable symphony with a detachment only fitting to the vanguard. As he pondered another nuanced ruse fraught with expedients, he came to an end of the escalator and disappeared.

Chris Forhan

ESSAY: WHEN I SAY "I": POETS' USE OF THE FIRST PERSON

At a writers' conference a few years back, a poet of some repute complained about the habit we have gotten into of referring to a poem's "speaker." "'Speaker' isn't quite right," he argued. "There has to be a better term." If he knew what that term is, he wasn't saying, but many contemporary poets share his discomfort. Is a poem always "speaking," exactly? Might we be more accurate, in some cases, to refer to the poem's "thinker"? Its "feeler"? Its "nervous system"? And is the voice of the poem necessarily a singular, identifiable voice? Maybe we should talk about the poem's "center of attention."

If we are evasive on this matter, however, it is a necessary evasiveness, especially when we are talking about a first person poem that works—that moves and haunts us. The "I" in such a poem is essentially unknowable, or at least incompletely knowable.

When I write a poem that uses the first person singular, I hardly ever feel that I am referring to myself, exactly. In fact, part of what compels me to finish the poem is that I want to be surprised by what is on the mind of this "I"; I want to try to figure out who this "I" might be. The poem becomes a record of this attempt, and, if the poem is successful, the attempt at least partially fails. Still, whatever self the "I" refers to is real. It exists in the poem, but not only in the poem. It is constructed by the language, but I recognize it from elsewhere. I've met it while walking down a darkened, vacant street; I've met it in a restaurant, invisible in the empty seat beside me; I've met it in dreams.

We know what recent language theory would say about this. Deconstruction sees a gap between word and meaning, an imprecise relationship between signifier and signified. Thus, it is questionable whether we can read a lyric poem as the expression of a coherent "I." A poem is not spoken but written, and to write is to give control over to language, which doubles or erases its meanings as it goes, the self's intentions be damned.

But if the self that a poem professes to express is necessarily a product of the poem's language, and if language itself is contingent upon various social, historical, and cultural conditions, we nonetheless read poems to be reminded of what it feels like to be human, what it feels like to have a self, whatever that self might be. At least I do. It is useful to question the degree to which poetic language can express an identifiable and coherent self, but it is reductive to conclude that poetic expression is therefore, above all else, suspect.

Language *does* have meanings. It *does* communicate. Let's say that, while attending a dinner party, I announce that I believe I am experiencing a heart attack. Upon hearing this, the assembled guests might immediately note that the word "heart" is shadowed by the similar-sounding word spelled "h-a-r-t," which refers to a deer, and that in using the word "attack," I have unconsciously alluded to the concept of *tacking* objects to bulletin boards (themselves a kind of text) and that it is a short leap from the notion of the deer to that of other hoofed animals, so my statement is equally an unintended reference to the childhood game of *pinning* (tacking) the tail on the donkey— a subject I didn't have in mind, exactly, when I spoke but one that is worth pondering, specifically as it represents the willingness of a hegemonistic western culture to domesticate, objectify and reconstruct for its own ethnocentric purposes the natural world—a willingness, indeed, born of the narrow perspective suggested by the very blindfold traditionally donned by he or she whose task it is to pin the tail on the donkey.

Still, while all this deconstruction is going on, I hope someone at the table calls 911.

I am finally not very interested in poems that merely bring me the old news that words mean less or more than we think they do. We live in a poetic age that prizes the fragment, discontinuity, and aggressive indeterminacy—often at the expense of, or even while holding in contempt, lyricism. But, however worthy its desire to reflect the shifting, elusive nature of reality, any aesthetic uninterested in the ways that language embodies feeling is fatally crippled. We still sing amid the rubble.

Some of our better contemporary poets do not pretend to speak directly out of a static, definable self, but they also do not dismiss entirely the capacity of language to communicate subjective human experience. They use the pronoun "I," but the identity of that "I" is often vague—and it is typically not, or at least not merely, the poet. Instead, in using a first person speaker, these writers interrogate the nature of the self and confront its ultimate mystery. Their poems do not use language merely to remind us that language is insufficient; instead, they employ the ambiguity and indirectness of poetic expression to come as close as possible to conveying the complicated and bewildering quality of subjective experience. These are poets who, in saying "I," know that there is something at stake when they do, who know that to write the poem is to fumble after the "I," following where it leads—and to follow the "eye" where it looks. As Charles Wright says, "The 'I' is the great turnkey for the poem, the great opener. Almost all the 'great' poems—from Sappho to Yeats—are in the 1st person singular. Especially since the Romantics, it's hard to have a 'vision' if you're not in it, and it's not in you."

The "I" of the sort of poem I am thinking of may be born out of autobiography, but it is also half-created—recognizable from our experience in the world but quickened into speech only in the realm of the poem because it is the compressed, gestural, musical language of poetry that comes closest to saying what cannot be said. Others, of course, have thought about this. As Marvin Bell puts it, "The I in the poem is not you but someone who knows a lot about you." Rimbaud famously proclaimed in a letter, "It's wrong to say: I think. Better to say: I am thought . . . . *I* is an *other*" (100). I am reminded, too, of a peculiar statement the actor Anthony Hopkins made once in an interview that, upon reflection, suggests nothing so much as the disinterestedness that Keats argued is so important to the true artist. When the interviewer persisted in asking him probing autobiographical questions, Hopkins stumbled, paused, and finally explained, "My life is none of my business."

For poets whose work, in the 1950s and '60s, was the first described as "confessional"—writers such as Lowell, Plath, Berryman, and Sexton—their lives were very much their business. No matter the (considerable) stylistic differences among them, these writers shared the poetic project of treating intimate, sometimes disturbing autobiographical material in a way that did not shut readers out of the poem's concerns. Their challenge was to transform the private life into public art. The fields cultivated by these poets have continued, in the decades since, to be tilled by writers whose work is energized by the urgent claims of the autobiographical; however, such work also risks—if it focuses on an "I" that seems merely to be the poet, un-transformed and unexamined, speaking out of his or her own personal life—being limited in its vision and irrelevant to the reader. A poet working in the confessional mode must be wary of writing, to borrow Stephen Yenser's terms in his criticism of Lowell's late work, "gossip," not "gospel" (qtd. in Hamilton 432).

Decades before the work of the first generation of confessional poets, William Carlos Williams, in poems employing stripped-down diction and natural speech rhythms, was showing how a poet might convey his intimate life with immediacy and tension and without the enervating effect that can result from the inclusion of private details that seem of import only to the poet, not to the poem. In "Danse Russe" and "Waiting," for instance, the "I" of the poems is Williams, but it also could be anyone. Of her own use of first person, Emily Dickinson explained, "When I state myself, as the Representative of the verse—it does not mean—me—but a supposed person" ("To T. W. Higginson" 176). Williams' speakers have the whiff of that supposed person about them. Theirs is the voice of someone—it could be almost anyone—caught in the act of thinking.

"Danse Russe"

If I when my wife is sleeping
and the baby and Kathleen
are sleeping
and the sun is a flame-white disc
in silken mists
above shining trees,—
if I in my north room
dance naked, grotesquely
before my mirror
waving my shirt round my head

and singing softly to myself:
"I am lonely, lonely,
I was born to be lonely,
I am best so!"
If I admire my arms, my face,
my shoulders, flanks, buttocks
against the yellow drawn shades,—

Who shall say I am not
the happy genius of my household? (86-87)

This poem's speaker is a husband and father; considering the craving for freedom and solitude in the poem, that fact is relevant—but the poem doesn't give us any more information about this particular marriage than we need in order to make that connection. Who, though, we might ask, is Kathleen? It doesn't matter. The man in the poem is, on one level, Williams himself, and Kathleen was a domestic worker who lived with the Williams family for a time. But *not* knowing that fact, I would argue, does not prevent us from understanding the poem. In fact, it *helps*. The poem is a single sentence, a burst of thought, a brief revery; it is the internal musing of someone who doesn't need to explain to himself who is living in his house—and the intensity of that revery is underscored by the off-handed way the poet mentions "Kathleen" without comment and moves along. This light touch, this naturalness, makes the "I" of the poem sound both genuine and appealingly mysterious.

A similar sort of expansive use of the first person occurs in Williams' poem "Waiting":

"Waiting"

When I am alone I am happy.
The air is cool. The sky is
flecked and splashed and wound
with color. The crimson phalloi
of the sassafras leaves
hang crowded before me
in shoals on the heavy branches.

When I reach my doorstep
I am greeted by
the happy shrieks of my children
and my heart sinks.
I am crushed.

Are not my children as dear to me
as falling leaves or
must one become stupid
to grow older?
It seems much as if Sorrow
had tripped up my heels.
Let us see, let us see!
What did I plan to say to her
when it should happen to me
as it has happened now? (163-64)

Here, again, are Williams and his family; nonetheless, again, the poem works no matter who we imagine the speaker to be. The "I" of "Waiting" is characterized by a sort of transparency; although he talks a lot about himself—although he is engaged in a private meditation—the poem never becomes unnecessarily private. In fact, as with "Danse Russe," the moves the poem makes that emphasize the intimacy of the meditation help draw us into the poem, not close us out. It is the poem's last four lines that I am especially interested in. "Let us see, let us see!" Williams writes. We might expect, in such an intimate, meditative poem, that the line would read, "Let *me* see, let *me* see." The shift into the first person plural is like a change of key; it introduces a bemused, even vaguely comic, note. For a moment, we hear the controlled voice of the doctor who says to the patient, "So how are we today? Let us take a look under that bandage, shall we?" The poem's language has become a little odd, as if the speaker is beginning to put a slight distance between himself and his subject—the oddness coming from the fact that the subject is, of course, himself. Earlier in the poem, the speaker has mentioned his "children"; he has not simply called them "they." In the poem's last sentence, however, he refers, obliquely, to "her."

This is a move comparable to the one Williams makes in "Danse Russe" when he mentions "Kathleen." In this case, we understand that "her" means the wife; the simple pronoun is all we need, and the entrance of the wife into the poem so suddenly and so late and in only that small word "her" makes the poem feel even more intimate and intense, more like something overheard, not explained. By these last four lines of the poem, the language has become unsettled; one can hear it even in the rhythm, with the predominance of mono-syllables and the stilted syntax. By the time the speaker refers to what has happened "to me," we can't be blamed for wondering just what that "me" is. This is a poem that does not presume to understand the self, but it does record what it is like to have one.

Two more recent poets, Charles Simic and Anne Carson, often center their poems around an "I," but they use distinctive strategies to suggest that this self is somehow a projected and impersonal one—if not always completely fictional, at least insufficiently knowable. Their first person speakers can therefore seem strangely veiled. Details in Simic's work can sometimes be connected to specific experiences in his life—for instance, his childhood in Yugoslavia during World War II, his emigration to the United States, his experiences in New York City as a young adult, and his marriage—but it is usually a mistake not to distinguish between Simic and the first person speakers of his poems. His "I" is typically a shadowy self, a possible self, a stranger—a self that exists somehow in the middle ground between language and the ineffable. As Simic put it in an interview, "[F]or me there is no *one* 'I.' 'I' is many. 'I' is an organizing principle, a necessary fiction, etc. Actually, I'd put more emphasis on consciousness, that which witnesses but has no need of a pronoun" (*The Uncertain Certainty* 67). The use of an almost cipher-like first person speaker is in accord with Simic's notion that poetry isn't so much about the poet's self as about all selves, or about some essential selfness (however cryptic or absurd) that is shared by all humans. "Poetry is the archeology of the self," he has said. "The bits and pieces one keeps digging up belong to the world—everybody's world. It's a paradox that has always amused me. Just when you think you're most subjective, you meet everybody else" (Weigl 210).

The poem "Cameo Appearance" is about the anonymous human self: the self either without a meaningful, knowable identity or with an identity that has been blotted out by powerful, impersonal forces.

"Cameo Appearance"

I had a small, nonspeaking part
In a bloody epic. I was one of the
Bombed and fleeing humanity.
In the distance our great leader
Crowed like a rooster from a balcony,
Or was it a great actor
Impersonating our great leader?

That's me there, I said to the kiddies.
I'm squeezed between the man
With two bandaged hands raised
And the old woman with her mouth open
As if she were showing us a tooth

That hurts badly. The hundred times
I rewound the tape, not once
Could they catch sight of me
In that huge gray crowd,
That was like any other gray crowd.

Trot off to bed, I said finally.
I know I was there. One take
Is all they had time for.
We ran, and the planes grazed our hair,
And then they were no more
As we stood dazed in the burning city,
But, of course, they didn't film that.

"That's me there," the speaker says to "the kiddies" as he watches the film of a wartime scene. Who is this "me," though? This is one of the many instances in Simic's work of a recurring theme that he refers to in another poem as "the great secret which kept eluding me: / knowing who I am" ("The Initiate" 59). The speaker in "Cameo Appearance" knows he "was there" and is intent on proving it to the children with visual evidence, as if his relevance and identity will be assured if he can do so. However, he can't find himself. He has been erased—and what has been erased was of little value to begin with; as the poem announces in its opening line, "I had a small, nonspeaking part . . . ." The speaker is important not as a distinctive character so much as a representative of all humans, and humans in this poem are irrelevant and disposable; all of "[b]ombed and fleeing humanity" implicitly has a "small, nonspeaking part." The questioning of the meaning and truth of identity continues with the lines "In the distance our great leader / Crowed like a rooster from a balcony. / Or was it a great actor / Impersonating our great leader?" The only thing that seems certain in this poem, the only fact that can be recorded, is the suffering of humans who are impotent to protect themselves against modern, impersonal weapons of brutality. Tellingly, it is this suffering and these weapons, certainties that they are—not the poem's speaker—which are depicted with precise images:

> . . . the man
> With two bandaged hands raised
> And the old woman with her mouth open
> As if she were showing us a tooth
> That hurts badly. . . .

> We ran, and the planes grazed our hair.

Were it not for the one mention of the planes and the film, this could be a war in almost any place and any century. Typical of the images in a Simic poem, the descriptions of the man and woman here are specific in their visual detail yet also generic, even archetypal, in their feel, as if these two humans are recurring characters in a story that has been told for ages. One male and one female representative of the bombed and fleeing masses, they might be what became of Adam and Eve long after they were kicked out of Paradise. It is not, then, finally the speaker of the poem who is the central character; the central character is any of us—anyone who might be fleetingly glimpsed among the "gray crowd / That was like any other gray crowd."

The speaker of "Cameo Appearance" is a victim of forces larger than himself, whether forces of the state or of the cosmos; he is absent from official history. His is a familiar voice in Simic's poetry—the voice of a self that lacks definition and coherence, the voice of a floating, questioning, bemused consciousness. In what can be read as an ars poetica—one that has as its basis a suspicion of ultimate claims about individual identity—Simic once wrote, "Others pray to God; I pray to chance to show me the way out of this prison I call myself" (*Orphan Factory* 46).

The self-professed subject for Simic is, as he has said, "always 'truth,' but not the literal one" (Weigl 222). This leads to poems with a surreal and mythic bent. One would be hard-pressed to call Anne Carson a surrealist, but she, like Simic, is not content with a conventional realistic approach. Her lyrics and narratives tend to be fragmented, even collage-like, in their mixing of various genres and modes of discourse, which contributes to the sense that the poems' speakers have uncertain knowledge of themselves and the signifi-cance of their experience.

And who are Carson's speakers? Whose consciousness is it that the poems record? It is not much help to our understanding of Carson's poems to read their speakers as being simply the poet herself. As Carson said in a recent interview:

> I've often, while [using the first person], wondered, "Who is this *I*?" It's not identical with me. It's continuous but yet constructed. I don't exactly know how to define that quality that's in *I*. It's all mixed up with autobiography, but it's not the same . . . because I don't simply want to tell what is. I want to tell what is with all the radiations around it of what could be. So it's not simply a tran-scription of anything that actually happened but what actually happened, plus all the thoughts that one could think about it if one could walk around it, stop time and walk around the moment. And once you add in all that gradation of the moment it's no longer the event. The event is just the raw material that goes into your obser-

vation of what you see when you walk around it. It could be any subject matter. (Gannon 29-30)

Carson, then, is a poet who prizes fidelity to truth and to the imagination (and perhaps does not see those two things as being in opposition to each other). She is interested in probing the subject of the self and circling around it without reaching for tidy explanations. Her poems, as a result, are, at least on the surface, formally messy. Her long poem *The Glass Essay* is an example. In telling the story of a failed love affair and her response to it, the poem's speaker mixes that narrative with several other tales: primarily the stories of a visit to her mother and of the life and work of Emily Bronte, but also briefer sub-plots involving her dreams, her psychotherapy sessions, and a visit to her ailing father in the hospital. She shifts abruptly from one narrative thread to another and from one mode of discourse to another; the general sense of disjunctiveness is also contributed to by her tendency to employ clipped, declarative sentences, a technique which often leaves ambiguous the connection between thoughts. In its gaps and veerings, the poem refuses the temptation to construct an easily comprehensible and coherent version of the self. It is an illustration of Hayden Carruth's claim that a poem's "genuine passion does not come from the constricted ego, which can only tie itself in knots and has no innate recourse but suicide. It comes from the transcended ego in an ecstasy of concern" (Miller 19).

In focusing on the pain of a ruptured romantic relationship and a problematic mother-daughter relationship, *The Glass Essay* is quite intimate and personal, yet it is wary of making claims about the nature of the self that experiences that pain. Although the poem's short first section is entitled "I," it subtly—with a single word—hints at the difficulty the poem will have defining just what that "I" is.

"I"

I can hear little clicks inside my dream.
Night drips its silver tap
down the back.

> At 4 A.M. I wake. Thinking
>
> of the man who
> left in September.
> His name was Law.
>
> My face in the bathroom mirror
> has white streaks down it.
> I rinse the face and return to bed.
> Tomorrow I am going to visit my mother. (1)

In the penultimate line, one would expect Carson to write, "I rinse *my* face." Her use of the impersonal article "the" suggests the distance between the speaker and a clear conception of herself—the self that fell in love with a man and then was damaged by his departure. This lack of certainty is suggested throughout the poem, so *The Glass Essay* can be read as a search for knowledge about the nature of the self and about the significance of the impact of experiences upon that self. However, by poem's end, the speaker has discovered no easy answers. Here are the last lines of the poem:

> Something had gone through me and out and I could not own it.
> "No need now to tremble for the hard frost and the keen wind.
>
> Emily does not feel them,"
> wrote Charlotte the day after burying her sister.
> Emily had shaken free.
>
> A soul can do that.
> Whether it goes to join Thou and sit on the porch for all eternity
> enjoying jokes and kisses and beautiful cold spring evenings,
>
> you and I will never know. But I can tell you what I saw.
> Nude #13 arrived when I was not watching for it.
> It came at night.
>
> Very much like Nude #1.
> And yet utterly different.
> I saw a high hill and on it a form shaped against hard air.

It could have been just a pole with some old cloth attached,
but as I came closer
I saw it was a human body

trying to stand against winds so terrible that the flesh was
     blowing off the bones.
And there was no pain.
The wind

was cleansing the bones.
They stood forth silver and necessary.
It was not my body, not a woman's body, it was the body of us all.
It walked out of the light. (38)

"Something had gone through me and out," she says, "and I could not own it." The experience that this 38-page poem has recounted and examined is finally summarized as being, vaguely, merely "[s]omething," and the fact of the speaker being unable to "own it" implies not simply that its existence within her was impermanent but that her knowledge of it must remain incomplete. Throughout the poem, the speaker describes various "naked glimpses of [her] soul" that she calls "Nudes." In the end, the final Nude is a figure whose bones "stood forth silver and necessary. / It was not my body, not a woman's body, it was the body of us all." The poem's investigation of the nature of the speaker's self as she has confronted intimate experiences peculiar to her has, paradoxically, culminated in this: a romantic vision of that self as being genderless, egoless, united with all of humanity. Such a notion echoes Emerson's belief in the capacity of the self to become a "transparent eye-ball," to transcend "all mean egotism," and to feel its essential connection with all things (1075). The idea of a shared humanity—and its attendant implication that there are essential human experiences that art can speak of—isn't very fashionable these days, but it is an idea with which some of our best poets sympathize. A poet does not have to share with Emerson a belief in a transcendent spiritual reality to believe in a universal *human* reality that can be suggested poetically. Galway Kinnell puts it this way, with a nod to Emerson' language:

Often a poem at least starts out being about oneself, about one's experience, a fragment of autobiography. But then, if it's really a poem, it goes deeper than personality. It takes on that strange voice, intensely personal yet common to everyone, in which all rituals are spoken. A poem expresses one's most private feelings; and these turn out to be the feelings of everyone else as well. The separate egos vanish. The poem becomes simply the voice of a creature on earth speaking. (6)

Carson's *The Glass Essay* transcends its private subject matter and becomes communal in part because of the "strange voice" in it that is nonetheless recognizably human. It is a voice whose signature is a clipped syntax that suggests at once an objective mind examining reality closely and volcanic emotions trying desperately to restrain themselves. This conflict is emphasized, too, by the poem's odd juxtaposition of modes of discourse and tone. In the following passage, one line barely articulates a feeling through monosyllabic words and a sentiment that might be drawn from a pre-teen's diary entry, but it is followed by a line whose understated, almost dismissive tone suggests the sound of the self turning away from—or apologizing for—its deepest concerns:

When Law left I felt so bad I thought I would die.
This is not uncommon. (8)

That guarded tone, that apparent veering away by the speaker from a confrontation with her inchoate and overwhelming emotions, is not an evasion; it is the sound of a self that is ambiguous and multiple in its concerns and conceptions. It is a tone that serves as a foil for the poem's more searing, emotionally bare passages, giving those sections the quality of hard-earned unveilings of difficult truths. It comes as something of a surprise, for instance, when, eleven pages into the poem, the speaker proclaims:

Everything I know about love and its necessities
I learned in that one moment
when I found myself

thrusting my little burning red backside like a baboon
at a man who no longer cherished me. (11-12)

The Glass Essay does not deny that an important function of
poetry is to examine and express the complicated nature of the interior
life, and it does not imply that such a goal cannot be achieved
through poetic expression. It does, however, persuade us that the
self is perhaps essentially unknowable—or at least that to discover
and define the self is no easy task, and that poetry can honor this
truth.

With the famously strange and shapeshifting work of John
Ashbery, one desires to get a toe-hold somewhere. One wants a firm
place from which to begin reading. Here is a passage from his poem
"Houseboat Days" that can be taken as a statement of purpose:

But I don't take much stock in things
Beyond the weather and the certainties of living and dying:
The rest is optional. To praise this, to blame that,
Leads one subtly away from the beginning, where
We must stay, in motion. (231)

If we "stay" yet are "in motion," we are going to be slippery prey
indeed, difficult to pin down. The motion of Ashbery's poetry occurs
in part through the seemingly random way he shifts pronouns—from
singular to plural, from first to second to third person. By remaining
in flux, Ashbery's poems refuse to settle into a particular angle of
vision or into a particular conception of reality. However, this does
not mean that Ashbery, as some of his critics would have it, glibly or
coyly avoids meaning and engagement with real experience. When
Ashbery's poetry is at its most persuasive and beguiling, it appears
to be willing to bet its life on whatever notion is crossing its mind at
the time, even if that notion will happen to be contradicted in the
next line. The poems therefore feel intensely subjective, as if they
record the very inner part of the self so separate from the social self
that it is egoless, the place in which subjectivity expands to include
not just the "I" but the "we" and the "you" and the "him," "her,"
and "they." Here is Ashbery's poem "Crazy Weather":

"Crazy Weather"

It's this crazy weather we've been having:
Falling forward one minute, lying down the next
Among the loose grasses and soft, white, nameless flowers.
People have been making a garment out of it,
Stitching the white of lilacs together with lightning
At some anonymous crossroads. The sky calls
To the deaf earth. The proverbial disarray
Of morning corrects itself as you stand up.
You are wearing a text. The lines
Droop to your shoelaces and I shall never want or need
Any other literature than this poetry of mud
And ambitious reminiscences of times when it came easily
Through the then woods and ploughed fields and had
A simple unconscious dignity we can never hope to
Approximate now except in narrow ravines nobody
Will inspect where some late sample of the rare,
Uninteresting specimen might still be putting out shoots, for all we
    know. (221)

Although he is unlike Whitman in many ways, Ashbery shares
with him a sense of the self's multitudinousness. Whitman says, "I
am large, I contain multitudes" (246); Ashbery finds room in his
poems for entire constellations of voices and perspectives. Also, as
Whitman was fond of mixing formal and demotic speech, mixing
high and low diction, so is Ashbery. We might say of his work that
the "I" is not so much the source of the poems as it is the target; it is
the magnet that, willy-nilly, pulls toward itself all sorts of images and
phrases. The "I" does not proclaim its beliefs; it collects possibilities.
That does not mean there is no "self" in an Ashbery poem. There is;
he is not merely playing word games. But the poems are interested
not so much in expressing the thoughts and feelings of an identifiable,
coherent self as in suggesting what it is like to *experience* thoughts
and feelings. The poems therefore move quickly and change course
suddenly.

In "Crazy Weather," Ashbery begins with a familiar vernacular expression—"It's this crazy weather we've been having"—and already the pronouns are introducing an odd sense of mystery. Who are "we"? we might ask. Moreover, what about that floating, unmoored pronoun "It"? *What* is "this crazy weather we've been having"? From there, though, the poem mainly continues to evade our attempts to connect the pronouns to any-thing or -one in particular. The "we" of the first line gives way to "People" in the fourth, then to "you" in the eighth and to "I" in the tenth before the poem circles back to "we" again in the last line. By then, however, one suspects the "we" aren't quite the same "we" the poem started with. The slipperiness of the pronouns mitigates against our inclination to read a literal narrative into the poem, to try to distinguish among characters and to place them in relation to each other. The poem is nonetheless about something more than mere language play; among other things, it is about the unlikeliness of ever detecting and conveying a stable truth, a subject that in Ashbery's work is given, by turns, a melancholy and a comic cast. "Crazy Weather" is about poetry, about perception, about longing—and there is an integrity to the way it circles *around* experience, the way it knows that, in a poem, the content of experience can only be gestured at. In remaining in motion, Ashbery's poem does not settle easily into a single stance, into an implication that the self can absorb experience, distill the truth from it, and then deliver that truth authoritatively in language. The self remains provisional, so the poem must, too, and the effect of this is a confrontation with what it feels like to be alive, not an evasion of it. As James Longenbach has written recently of Ashbery, "[H]is poems feel spoken even if they lack an easily identified speaker: their disjunctive manner does not preclude the fiction of the human subject, however intricately constructed the manner might suggest that fiction to be. This is why Ashbery's poems, no matter how obscure, no matter how aligned with what we think of as the dryer responsibilities of avant-garde poetry, are always ripe with pathos" (28).

When I, as a poet, say "I," that I is not me, exactly. I am not sure what it is, until the poem starts giving me clues. Sometimes the "I" is someone I'd like to be, or someone I hope I'm not, or someone I fear I might become if I keep living in this way, or someone I've fooled myself into thinking I was once. Sometimes it's a dog. If I presume to know too much about this "I" at the beginning, though, the poem is likely to fail; it will lack the energy and tension that come from mystery and discovery. For the poet, it is a good idea, while writing, to remain consciously ignorant for as long as possible—because, after all, we can trust that the place in us from which true poems come is never ignorant. Two centuries ago, Thomas Carlyle wrote, "Unconsciousness is the sign of creation. . . . So deep, in this existence of ours, is the significance of mystery" (qtd. in Abrams 217). This is old news but worth repeating. The self, no matter our various notions about it, ultimately keeps its secrets. That is one of the best reasons to write and read poetry. In one of her many poems exploring the outer reaches of consciousness—examining, in other words, what it is like to be a thinking and feeling self—Emily Dickinson describes how "I, and Silence," are "some strange Race / Wrecked, solitary, here" (#280 129). Perhaps the self exists most fully in silence. But if this "strange race"—this I, and this silence—can speak, its language is surely poetry.

נ נ נ

Works Cited

Abrams, M. H. *The Mirror and the Lamp: Romantic Theory and the Critical Tradition*. Oxford: Oxford UP, 1953.

Ashbery, John. *Selected Poems*. New York: Viking, 1985.

Bell, Marvin. "32 Statements about Writing Poetry (Work in Progress)." *The Writer's Chronicle* Special Commemorative Issue 2002. 13.

Carson, Anne. *The Glass Essay. Glass, Irony, and God*. New York: New Directions, 1995. 1-38.

Dickinson, Emily. #280 ("I felt a Funeral, in my Brain"). *The Complete Poems of Emily Dickinson*. Ed. Thomas H. Johnson. Boston: Little, Brown, 1960. 128-129.

---. "To T. W. Higginson." July 1862. Letter 268 of *Emily Dickinson: Selected Letters*. Ed. Thomas H. Johnson. Cambridge: Harvard UP, 1986. 175-176.

Emerson, Ralph Waldo. *Nature. The Norton Anthology of American Literature*. Ed. Nina Baym et al. 5th ed. Vol. 1. New York: Norton, 1998. 1072-1101.

Gannon, Mary. "Ann Carson: Beauty Prefers an Edge." *Poets and Writers* March/April 2001. 26-33.

Hamilton, Ian. *Robert Lowell: A Life*. New York: Random House, 1982.

Kinnell, Galway. *Walking Down the Stairs: Selections from Interviews*. Ann Arbor: U Michigan P, 1978.

Longenbach, James. "Disjunction in Poetry." *Raritan* 20.4 (Spring 2001). 20-36.

Miller, Matthew. "An Interview with Hayden Carruth." *The Writer's Chronicle* Sept. 2001. 12-19.

Rimbaud, Arthur. Letter to Georges Izambard. 13 May 1871. *Arthur Rimbaud: Collected Works*. Trans. Paul Schmidt. New York: Harper, 1976. 100-101.

Simic, Charles. "Cameo Appearance." *Walking the Black Cat*. San Diego: Harcourt Brace, 1996. 6.

---. "The Initiate." *The Book of Gods and Devils*. San Diego: Harcourt Brace, 1990. 59-61.

---. *Orphan Factory: Essays and Memoirs*. Ann Arbor: U Michigan P, 1997.

---. *The Uncertain Certainty*. Ann Arbor: U Michigan P, 1985.

Weigl, Bruce, ed. *Charles Simic: Essays on the Poetry*. Ann Arbor: U Michigan P, 1996.

Whitman, Walt. *Complete Poetry and Collected Prose*. New York: Library of America, 1982.

Williams, William Carlos. *The Collected Poems of William Carlos Williams*. Ed. A. Walton Litz and Christopher MacGowan. Vol. 1. New York: New Directions, 1986. 2 vols.

Wright, Charles. Letter to the author. 6 May 2002.

Richard P. Gabriel

ESSENCE OF MEMORY

when it came right down
to it
people left/walked out

horror
left in the dust

down stairs
past stares
what the mad makers

never imagined
was time
to walk away

    ₪

I bought a furnace
to keep
warm this Winter

forgetting the fires
of people

    ₪

there was a fountain
wrapped around the world

made of smoke
and up it
went

    ₪

people made of smoke
walked out
walked away
left us in the dust

Richard P. Gabriel

LESSON

Now a puzzling example!
Let's examine the dog barks.

The contextual analysis of bark
to detect the nuclear
does not add more information
due to the previous example

with head, but its context refers to a cry
that reveals the existence
of two contextual subject classes
that may match with bark.

—the human being class ("the dog barks")
and the animal class ("let's examine")—

Two contexts emerge
depending either on the animal
or the human being
such as animal cry
or human cry
as in the boy barks
to the moon!

Richard Garcia

HOLLYWOOD

This poem is not about itself, not about sailing
in a paper boat across a sea of intransitive verbs.
This poem does not know what an intransitive verb is.
It is not about sailing across your belly with my tongue
until I bump into the silver ring in your navel.
This poem is trying not to think about the silver ring
in your navel, not to think of its tiny skull face
that I can only see if I leave my glasses on.
It's diving underwater with open eyes.
It's pulling myself down a ladder rung by rung down
the page until I am sitting on the bottom of a swimming pool
but still able to breathe. The pool must be in Hollywood
because here comes Esther Williams and Fernando Lamas
in the prime of their lives swimming side by side
barely disturbing the surface of the pool—
backstroke, butterfly, crawl and suddenly the pool
is lined with towers of spray and scissoring ladies
of the aquacade in white bathing suits, all of them hanging on
to the edge of the pool, each with one leg in the air, foot arched,
toes pointed—a good time for you and me to slip away
barely disturbing the surface of this poem,
leaving the scratch, scratch of pen against paper far behind us
and there is only the sound of our breathing—
and with my face pressed into your hair, I ask you,
What do you call this kind of poem?
Ask me about the ocean, you answer, I don't know about pools.

Richard Garcia

NOT BAD FOR A HERMAPHRODITE

The poem was scrambled during transmission.
Previously, it had been tied to a gate and disemboweled.
Some said it was a hermaphrodite
whose secret name was suspected of being an anagram
of a supernatural being, a quadriplegic
God, fond of anyone who dressed Goth.

The poem could sing the entire libretto of Faust in Goth.
It could hum like a cherry V8 transmission
in a loaded '56 Chevy, it was, however, quadriplegic
and four of its stanzas were immobile—disemboweled
and deveined. It had chutzpa and a gram
of old fashioned moxie, not bad for a hermaphrodite.

In fact, it was titled "Not Bad for a Hermaphrodite."
In days of old it was chanted by drunken Goths
who thought its power was that it was an anagram
of something really important but lost in transmission.
The true truth of the universe unfortunately disemboweled,
disheveled and discarded on the road like a quadriplegic

marauder who couldn't admit he was quadriplegic.
Why was the poem hermaphrodite?
Because it was male and female, disemboweled,
held up by exterior struts of language like a gothic
cathedral, for it needed no vowels, it was pure transmission
and was just one word of an infinite license plate anagram.

Or was it one word of an orgasmic anagram?
The poet was fabled as a great lover, although quadriplegic.
The attention of his tongue, it was said, was direct transmission
to goddess-hood, pleasures beyond what contortionist hermaphrodites
strapped to vibrating washing machines during spin cycle by soapy Goths
could ever know, even if all inhibitions were disemboweled.

The poem would survive, even disemboweled,
for an alphabet of leaves flashing in wind was its anagram.
It could be stomped on by barbarians, savages, Goths.
It could sit upright on a blunt, oiled stake, be squashed by quadriplegic
elephants, and never recited by eunuchs or hermaphrodites
at weddings in India. Although invisible, its apogee was transmission.

Let it lay disemboweled in a vacant lot like a quadriplegic
Cadillac, let its anagram be garbled by poetically correct hermaphrodites—
the poem outlives theorists, deconstructing Goths, and its own transmission.

J.F. Garmon

AUTUMN DRUNK

But, no, not but, and, the right conjunction, and,
yes, and, it fits, starved luxury, mango time, and
the stubborn heart aches, gray trees turn green,
and we are drenched by summer rain, and blame
the gold silk those courtiers wore in ancient China,
Marco Polo mixing with the common folk, and
always looking for the just right woman, green
eyes, jewels luscious like frosted oranges, and
no wonder he stayed for seventeen years, and
got back in time to be on the losing side in war,
but the emperor was generous, set him free, and
he let his servants carry him miles through marsh
and desert, slowly past farms and rivers, boats
adrift in the free nights, and no one ever would
think someday it would be so like this, and so
overjoyed as Li Po drinking the last wine, and
the season becoming one bird singing, drunk
on the tangles of infinite questions.

Eric Gelsinger

STEAM
OR, LUCK

It had to do with looking at myself in the mirror and then putting
my clothes on without turning the light on.
It had to do with standing by an empty doorframe between rooms,
trying to see around night corners.
It had to do with never wanting to be alone; my most beautiful
experiences happen alone.
It had to do with the timing of things.

(he and I) are sleeping together, although we are not women.

emotions all silence,
lonely and bony legs; tapered rain drops are monotonously long,
and this hiss of their spear-fall outside, while I'm warm in bed,
makes me wonder.

the dream after death.
the silence in chest.
next in bed.

Reginald Gibbons

SUMMER

Under a front-yard being in full
Infinitely varied leaf—each, no matter
How imperfect, perfectly maple—
I wait, while at an angle to
The upright world rain
Begins to fall and vapor
From the hot wetted street rises
Through and against the rain,

Two motions interpenetrating,
Two metaphors proposing different ideas.

Meanwhile, dipping as the drops of rain
Strike them, this year's leaves say,
"As long as each of us lives, we live—
Whether each form of us is fully
Itself or stunted or eaten by
One creature or by another cut
Or by you sentenced."

Cloud-mist around the earth-bound.
Some idea, at last, where only
An attitude usually is.

"What has been the moment of your being—
You that think? Is your thinking being
The fullness of the form of you?"

Within hearing of a nearby synod
Of some hundreds of stamens convened
For silent sessions day and night
And nodding nay and yea while rain-being
Falls and mist-being rises,
I hesitate to answer.

Joy Gladding

SPROUTING GRASS MOON

Sometimes just opening
a window
to hear the air moving
is enough

                        not even wind

sometimes after making love
to lie very still
and listen for the slightest

shift

the wildness

                 retreating

the tongue coming
so civilly
to rest.

Elton Glaser

DAMAGE CONTROL

1

In this cool June, the lilies rot from
Standing water,
And snails horn themselves across the yard,
Smear on the underside of
Wet curls.

What can I wring from this
Spoiled garden,
Or beguile from the gauzy air?
I tunnel into the afternoon
And find

A dirty shade to sleep in, a ruck
Of sheets
Creasing the hard bed, each dream
A hinge that opens all the
Valves and portals.

2

We've lived through the leg-of-mutton sleeve,
The striped bustle,
And other deep impediments of plush
That stay the sparks and keep
The engine cold.

So many folds and sashes in the past!
Now we've gone
Beyond the tease of feathers, slow seep
Down the catwalk to a kink of
Sheers and heels.

Let the belly have its way—
Dark elegance
Of the pelt and groove, loose
Permission where the moist
Mysteries nest.

3
Above the waist, below the seam—
Nothing breeds
In the distant barrens of the body
(Though I could love you
Hand to mouth).

The muscle that once closed to hold me
—Control, control—
Slackens in the heat, and you back off
From this stiff bravado, this
Snare of grace.

When the nerves fail, folie à deux comes down
To one—
The night goes dry, knee-deep in moondust,
And all the stories seal themselves
In stone.

Rachel Hadas

THE NAP AND THE GENTLEMAN CALLER

Who is waiting for me, tall and solemn,
carrying isolation like a flame
cupped in his hands against a gust of wind?
Death in his straw hat. Death, I know your name.

A cottage, no, a cellar, no, a bunker
dark and dim. We writers lock the doors,
make tea. The place is bigger than I'd thought;
presently we break up into pairs.

Outside is courtly Death, not far away,
patiently standing with his burning eyes.
Unwillingly I wave: "I'll meet you later."
First other obligations loom—goodbyes

to friends I've known since childhood, sitting here,
quartet of pensioners who look at me
with the indifference of a window pane,
transparently as water, when I try

to speak to them. Whereas old dapper Death
(impeccably attired, crisp straw hat,
seersucker jacket, polished saddle shoes)
looks steadily my way, prepared to wait

one summer afternoon of tousled sleep,
sheer veil drawn over vistas of desire,
while in the next room voices rise and fall,
playwrights conferring on the other side of the wall.

Shauna Hannibal

AN ANNUNCIATION

You would have called me yesterday,
if you knew what practicing grass in the wind
means to me, who is already
hearing midges, hundreds
of them, wings beating fast.
It's obvious I don't want to talk,
that's fine, but according to the chart
your body's blazing. What you're saying
is being contravened
by a deity,
you thought I had
the right to know.

Shauna Hannibal

STAY,

it's too early.
More cause to be troubled

                         on the rim

of the place,
don't leave so soon.

All birds alight all wrong this ache

                         when the sorry shines through.

Plenty wire springs

                         the full-on reverie of a mind

paneled.

Exit,   then the music,
yes, that's right.

Matt Hart

SCARY ROWBOAT

Surprise! says the plumber with aplomb
from the basement, These veins I install
transport fluids to the sea.
Shouldn't that be enough to comfort us
in our times of great retention?

We pay for the landlord's toilet. We live
in the landlord's brothel. At one time, too,
my favorite restaurant was a brothel.
Now they serve pasta next to bathtubs and beds.

I think of the prostitutes hitting their heads,
the customers careening to pieces. And later,
for dessert, I butcher Breton,
Convulsions will be beautiful or will not be
(I sing to the beauty across from me).
If more coffee may kill me, yes, more coffee please,
but we, and our cups, remain empty.

And what else is beautiful, she asks?
—A root canal flowing, a church organ failing.
What is failing? —A swan song
balanced in the spine of a book. Why
are you crying? —The oil-slick mangle
of life ever-ending. We carry our guts in a sack.

Matt Hart

AT THE MOMENT I AM UNWILLING

to consider the other inside
of my skull, so I lean over the sink
and witness my interrogation by goldfish.
The way the questioning begins, so wide out

beyond the stars, should be enough
to convince me to stop telling the truth,
but what else am I going to say? I am
the back of a hollowed-out theater, and anyway

the movie that isn't playing would've been merely
flash: sparklers at sunset, glitter at dawn.
It isn't so much the line of inquiry as the lack of it.
My abdomen seems mostly sewn up. Once in a while

a candy apple oozes over the hood of my car, but
otherwise nothing spectacular. For instance
I hold my breath between two fingers and wilt
into the amplified lack of particular circumstances.

No one does his banking. No one walks her dog.
I wish and the wishes appear to me as shoddy brown
leaves on the workroom floor. Sorry, by the way,
to the mole I broke in the yard. Another dead thing

shut out of its misery. The question then
becomes, Why resist wishful thinking at all
when life is a cabaret of spleens and propellers? One
beam of light fires onto the screen, as elsewhere

a lonely bulb burns out in the kitchen. My wife feels
sorry for the distress this causes me. Translated:
a tarpaper mousetrap prevails. I set sail
ten years ago for a new Byzantium, one

where the bare minimum of anything
is material to begin with again. Someone
has buried my parakeet feet. Now I can't
find the world. That's enough. End here.

Matt Hart

REVIEW:
TREMOLO by SPENCER SHORT
HarperCollins, 2001. $16.00

tremolo: n, pl -**los** [It fr. tremolo, tremulous, fr. L tremulus] (ca 1801) **1 a :** the rapid reiteration of a musical tone or of alternating tones to produce a tremulous effect **b :** vocal vibrato esp. when prominent or excessive **2 :** a mechanical device in an organ for causing a tremulous effect.

Spencer Short's book *Tremolo* opens with the line "One enters as one enters" and winds up 75 pages later, "lost on the music-boat of youth, sighing *justice.—ice. Ice.* Ice." In between, a world is laid open like a chest-of-hearts: for every beat, a non-beat, for every tremor, a drone, for every word spoken—another word spoken. Tremolo indeed, esp. dictionary definition **1b**, which speaks of vocal vibrato, both prominent and excessive. The voice in Short's poems, too, both prominent and excessive. "Around here, my dears," jabs the speaker in "Der Neuen Gedichte," "no one sleeps." It's true, too. These poems seem to have been up all night talking. They're monologues of a sort, where talk necessarily takes center stage, but it's a particular kind of talk: neurotic, obsessive, ever-questioning. Truly, the philosophical and psychological urges in these poems are as prominent as the poetic ones. And it's the back and forth between these various ways of approaching the word, the self, and the world that creates the tremulous effect which is not only the book's name-sake, but the primary force at the heart of its poems.

One enters Short's book as one enters any book, for any number of reasons, and exits through the last line "lost" and "sighing" over the italicized "ice" in italicized "justice." That is, the "just ice," which melts, and "just words," which eventually fade away with fashion, or time or death. Here, too, is the idea that spoken language is devious in the way it's both cold (it says what it says) and alive (because it says more than what it says depending on how far one is willing to break it down, turn it around, and poke it with a stick). Reading these poems one is distinctly aware of the fact that Short, whatever else he seems to be talking about, implying and/or trying to put over, is always also talking about the language he's using to do it. For example, looking again at the book's final line, Short repeats ice three times in three different ways (italicized "*ice*" then italicized, capitalized "Ice" and finally capitalized, non-italicized "Ice.") suggesting at least three ways of thinking about the word: as spoken, as typography, as metaphor. One enters as one enters, but in the end one is bound to be something else, something that ceases to enter: lost with a head full of music or a body full of sighs, one eventually confronts the final moment and goes cold. Capital Ice. No italics. No speech. No language.

₪ ₪ ₪

But Short isn't death obsessed, I am. In fact, for him, just the opposite is the case—and this gets back to the neurotic, talky part (Short's, not mine)—these poems are packed with life. They defy the end by continuing to talk. They're dense effusions, moving in close to describe the world and then backing up to consider the words used to describe it before moving in close again, etc. Thus, poetic tremolo occurs as the poems move back and forth between the words and their analysis. For example, look at this passage from "Poem":

> Okay. A boy has lost his dog & so.
> Said dog becomes free-floating,
> a disloyal signifier amid an afternoon's quiet decompression.
> For the first time loss unfolds its beach chairs in said boy's mind.
> Erects its fort too close to water. The sky is everywhere   (16)

Here Short moves fleetly from the talky, matter-of-factness of sentences like "Okay" and "A boy has lost his dog & so," to the word "dog," then to the emotional language of loss, then to the beach, the boy's mind, water, and suddenly, as if by accident, "The sky is everywhere." The poem never stops considering things from different angles, which almost insures that eventually Short will surprise us. "The sky is everywhere." Yeah. The poem shifts like clouds.   What Short does amazingly well here is to set a scene and then imagine its implications as metaphor, information, and philosophy almost simultaneously. In this way the poem works as both poetry and as instructions on how to read it. Another way of thinking about it is as a scene unfolding on several different levels at once: narratively (the boy loses his dog and then experiences for the first time an overwhelming sense of loss) emotionally (from the flatness of Okay to sadness over the lost dog to being alone and swallowed up under the sky), mechanically (as beach chairs unfold), grammatically (as sentences unfold). And the more I look at this passage, and Short's poems in general, the more things keep unfolding.

For instance, "dog & so" suggests "so & so"—a distance, a detachment, a pre-occupation with the generic, literary aspects of the dog as "dog," a word, a place holder for a particular dog, leading directly to "Said dog becomes free-floating." As a matter of fact, one might also describe a *dead dog* as free floating and maybe also as decompressed. Which, in its turn, reminds of the "depression" in "decompression," both in the word, and in the world: in the over-whelming image of a sky reflected in water, especially (worse) blue water—blue everywhere: blue poem, blue sky, blue boy without his so & so. Yes, let the signifiers float.

As Short writes later in the same poem:

Everything come running. Into. Everything bleeding into the other

This is the aesthetic, the rule, upon which "Poem" (16) and Short's whole book is based. But it's also the rule by which we read it. To get "Into" these poems one must be willing to move back and forth tremulously, between the "Everything come running" and the "Everything bleeding into the other."

Terrance Hayes

MAUSOLEUM

Well, let's get right to it: my parents live in a mausoleum. It's never too late for someone to kill someone else. No obit says of the recently dead: "He was cruel, he was low down and selfish, the world is brighter without him," but wouldn't that be great? In October the leaves pile up like wrapping paper on a Christmas afternoon. In January the lawn awaits its snow. Here, the sky still holds strips of the uncooked meat of sunset, you are not getting something for nothing. It is not all new or available for a limited time only. Here, one gets more things to get more things. When the blood exits, it doesn't return. And one day maybe you find a box of your mother's poems in the basement. Wouldn't that be great. And to do nothing! To grow huge and short-breathed doing nothing in a house of what-nots. Like the elderly. Like a childless couple with three cars. Like a house with a television in every room.

Terrance Hayes

SEABROOKS

I began
with dark water,
ripples made

by greased fingers;
my grandmother,

the yellow maiden
broken by goodbyes,
the flower-breeder

whose mouth
is a latched fence,

whose sons belch
hooch notes,
whose daughters

are wounded lipstick.
Once my grandmother's hair

was crimped & dyed
gold as the nails
of the young women

at the beauty school.
Once she was so young

she refused to marry.
She blessed her children
with a made up name.

While her daughters slept,
she wove braids

of rain into their hair.
Her suitors drank
by the untuned piano

When the cigarettes were done,
it was time to sing.

Someone played a melody
using only the black keys.
My cousins & I thought

the world had finished spinning,
but it had only been at rest.

My grandmother buried her bag
of pills in the yard
& green petals sprouted

from the sores behind her knees.
We began with the broken song

gurgling from a brook.

Dianna Henning

DUST

is where the cowboy gallops off,
a horse vanishing behind the brush.
The careless whirl of tiny particulars,
their rub against the northeasterly.

Born to get small. As though the foremost lesson
of life were *don't let too much pride*
pump you. And even if you wanted to swell,
the scarecrow-years inform you
that when it all comes down
what keeps you and your bones together
is a faint suspicion
one cannot do without the other.

Skin stretches to take up the slack. You go where
The bones go. The horse goes on with or without you.

David Hess

WHIRLED

Like Huysmans' Des Esseintes
to have the perfect library
of almost nothing
    something too beautiful
to read or touch not more
than once
      then to dream about it
for the rest of time

He admitted it
the truly great bored him
only the imperfect could sing
the impure   word-drops
condensations and shades
   of entire lives in a few lines
could satisfy him

the pollutant delicacy
irritant in time's steamroller tide
   jeweled nail
sticking out
lying in wait
     for the inflated tires
       of progress

George Higgins

Mingus

Everyone crowds the makeshift bandstand:
the younger couples dance
anywhere, squeeze forward
like a cheap special effect in a 50's Sci-Fi flick,
and demonstrate detachment like a bag of tacks, the
devil's cold fingers,
or saturation like smeared ink from a love letter.
A couple adjusts their Monet's "Waterlillies"
umbrella,
so they can observe their younger reflections.
Beads of water falling over the tarp,
the condensation rising
with the recycled roots, chords and tonics,
mingling among us this afternoon.

Jonathan Holden

TRANSITIVITY

It's tantalizing,
like a metaphor, or better say
the structure of a metaphor
to *carry across* the gap between
the pale germ of a jet
fleeing through the stratosphere
the streak behind
it and now the third term,
a crumpling echo
which comes seeping
down to us so
gently.
I remember watching
a guy in a gang
beat up another boy
smickety-smackety
who wouldn't wait in line
for a pool table
and his semi-hood named Jimmy,
the gang's spokesman, explaining to us
cheerfully *Some kid*
was giving us lip,
so Ernie roughed him up a little.
A sick gap in my gut.
Ernie was their fist.
The gang was Jimmy's
fist. Power is transitive.
There's a certain kind
of kiss, it's when my love's
tongue-tip is like
the pale blue tip
of an Ohio strike-

anywhere match, or
better say it
is the very tip of
the soft blue flame
of a Bunsen
burner. (Because we're
civilized we'll leave
case and its effect
implicit, let it
tantalize.)

Roy Jacobstein

MOTHS

—for Dean Young

These telemarketers are like God,
or feral cats, always there for you
at the worst moments. No, I don't
fancy a monthly box of navel oranges,
thank you, or pig's knuckles, liverwurst,
hearts of palm, not when it's almost time
for my Friday game of quoits. Why can't
I be the steady boatman of my dreams?
The breeze was blowing eddies of myrrh
beneath a slivered Mesopotamian moon.
Maybe it was frankincense. The princess
herself, all saffrons and silks, wafted
toward me, trailed by her tittering retinue.
My pole found purchase in the murky Tigris,
but then Red-Eye's blackboard-chalk shrieks
outside my window clawed me three millennia
back to this duplex, its vapors, its must,
its de-clawed housecats—and the moths,
the moths, all night the pitiless moths.
Someone told me ancient Egypt venerated cats,
but it wasn't Carrie, she's just calling
from *The Herald-Sun* to inquire if I want
weekend service. What impeccable timing—
the very moment my worn Random House
is telling me *kôr´e* is "a sculptured representation
of a young woman, particularly one
produced prior to the 5th Century B.C."
Aren't some things too uncanny for words?

Mark Jarman

AT THE BROADWAY EXIT

I rarely put the money out the window,
Call the sign-holder over with a dollar,
But when I do the thrill of breaking space,
The lowered glass between us, makes me dwell
All day on what I've done. He says, "God bless."
And what else can that money, which will buy
A bottle or a capsule or a bag,
What else could it have done except indulged me
As it has, folded, between my fingertips,
A signal cool as beckoning for music,
The soundtrack of our lives on radio,
Driving along famous in anonymity?
And yet it's not enough. I know it's not.
I wish I hadn't said a thing about it.

Halvard Johnson

VARIATIONS IN C

1.
First we drain all color from the sky
and then we strip the sea of its shimmer.
Moist residues abound, but certain
excesses of modern life refuse to unzip us.

2.
First she blindfolds him with a silken scarf
and then she lifts one breast to his mouth.
Winged furies spring from the corners
of the room, duly advised of both duties and rights.

3.
First clip-on bow ties and then cravats.
Sumptuous repasts on deck, then, at sunset,
ashore. To show any muscle,
we must make it perfectly clear that that is that.

4.
Some like it deep and slow at first, but then
require more flash and spontaneity
in the perpetual adjustments of their shredded
documentations, their unfolded folds.

5.
First, lift yourself about three inches off the floor
without offending the others. Then slowly
show us what you've got. No abstract nouns,
please. Just flesh and fur will do the trick.

Halvard Johnson

ALLEGED VARIATIONS

> "There are no answers. Then, of course, there are
> answers but the final answer makes the questions
> seem absurd, whereas the questions up until then
> seem more intelligent than the answers."
> —John Cage, "45' for a Speaker"

1.
There are no answers then. I don't know why
I thought there were. Do you? Even the atom begs
to be split. Two hazel eyes, like the twin

ends of a divining rod. We're left without fuel but with,
after all, a sense that our lives do matter.

2.
No answers then, of course. We contemplate the profound,
along with the mundane, soaked as it was in yellow light.

Lightly, the culture bends to the wind blowing up along
the river. The sky so pure you'd think

clarity was our base of operations. How can we
say, "like life itself," having no idea what that means?

3.
Then, of course, there are answers. They saw it happening
as they passed along the road beside that grove of trees.
Which was why, often, the cemeteries here are so calming.
"Look," I whispered. "Over there. Don't you see it?"

Returning at sundown, but not asking you to reveal anything
you didn't feel like revealing, I thought I might try once again

to win your approval and admiration. You kept to yourself,
though, taking your daily lessons down by the harbor.

4.
The final answer makes monkeys of us all,
say some, whose coastal hills shed great fervor
down upon the stark Pacific.
    California reduced
to a net of legal mayhem, visible to all
with eyes to look.

He had aplomb aplenty, but lacked, somehow, panache.
The silent house, meanwhile, dreamt of vacancy.

5.
The questions seem absurd, always. Avoidance
of silence becomes, for us, a spiritual quest,
living where we do at the intersection of fear and bravado.
Keeping one hand at all time on the steering wheel,
we find, at last, that "final image" should read
"sixth image," and that our indifference to all those miles
outstretched of barren desert terrain was in fact
well founded. We have gone off to live as we must,
no more intelligent than the answers we'd been seeking.

Kate Knapp Johnson

THE MEANING OF SIMPLICITY

—Title after Yannis Ritsos

It's nothing, not
to have you. Simple
as setting a table
for one, although
the candles are tricky—
this fire passes wick
to wick, the flame entirely
given away and still it remains, the same

golden fig above its waxy stem—
does every mystery
unlock another
more impervious,
but radiant mystery? A person

might unpetal this way, like
I know you, and then you open
into someone else again—just today
you stood on the steps that lead
to the usual sidewalk and seemed
a new and phenomenal form;
part-angel man, what are you

looking for? Always
the looking on your face, intent
as if something just quietly vanished—
was it there? (Was it lost?)
If it wasn't there
why are you looking?

Perhaps we are called,
something we dreamed of signals
and we hear (we think we hear?) and turn
towards what we thought
was the source, a sound
or voice, a clearing
from which to see, the stairs
leading down, if only
we had any certainty—

so you looked, this morning, surprised
as if you'd stumbled
on the secret that was never far
from you, but so impenetrable—
did you hear it approaching
or slipping away?

I would kiss you. For crying
out loud, I would
kiss you right on the mouth
if I thought it could lift
the ghost-glint from your eyes.
How simple, ingeniously
simple: our faces meet, the body
finally touched deeply enough. . .

No. This is the meaning
of simplicity: what is right here
before us: how
and what we experience—which is also
solitary—immanent, yes,
but invisible, nothing

we can ever hold on to—
is it only divined?: what we long for,
what we rush out into the street,
into the confusion of day, to find?—
it's unsayable, blinding,
our bright
white almostness.

Peter Johnson

THE DEEP FOOTPRINTS OF GOD

Are you ready for the smoke? Are you ready for the mirrors? I dreamt that half my ancestors were following railroad tracks into a mine, the other half watching football on TV. "It wasn't a dream, stupid, it was a wake-up call." Who said that? It could have been God. I found His big footprints in the backyard mud yesterday, haloed by Carmine's angel dust. "Existing is plagiarism," someone wrote. Think about that until your head hurts, until a darkness surrounds you like the shadow of a giant bat. The rain had stopped and I was outside, pleating a screen, trying to make an accordion for the wind. I was remembering that dream and how my father would crush walnuts in his bare hand. And there they were—my father's footprints. It was Easter and he had come to visit. He had taken the dog out to pee and was smoking angel dust with Carmine when he stepped into a patch of mud. Yet I still believe in the deep footprints of God, know that I'll stumble into them, that He'll part a cloud with His large right hand, look down on me and say, "Soldier on, boy, soldier on."

Jeffrey Jullich

MILD ACHES: AWARE BETTER PATH

mild aches. Aware better path
chances dismally declining for
snug, around shiny delicacies!
in fortune's jealous clutches.
propelled by the impact of hot
as long as speed flowed prices
and striped. One heel on iron
downhill foundations to carved
their credit subtracted. Dear
have missed you ever since vim
randomly selected from unified
miniature, smooth tip. Factor
bind. Prometheus, hero modern
denem never failed to activate
farewells wafted through trump
indivisible sections disintegr
neo-classical lilt to his gait
momentary transactions. Flacci
added that air of suave remove
goodbye to last year's optimis
up statistically likely. None
n't. Coating its luxurious kn
chained fast to a rock, pecked
fashion trends consummated raw

usually practice a minimum of twelve hour
After your unselfish
frantic because of an intolerable respect
Thanks to neighbors' curiosity
craft rewards. Sanguine confronted by Mr
Dogs leashed to bushes will
faulty wiring visible through peeling red

Members of an undergrou
inside her deceitful cunning.   Feminist
Blacklisted during
not a crumb for princes who invade," said
It is so. "Live
adopted, treated them better than his own
Protecting fin
looked up to the teacher as a great token
Those who would drea
due to unadvertised pleasures. Be docile
Silently bombarded
walls of cute psychic armor embittered by
Jacking the prongs onto
ringside seat. Clapping loudly to attrac
Passer-by caught frank wind of
seemingly unmoved as the storm beat quick
Shoved from the left, spat upon ideolo
sagging spaghetti? Strands of electrical
Are the ones divided lengthwise
devotes more attention to those disobedie
Refreshing to the consciou
try educated in strictest accordance with

Jeffrey Jullich

PAYING IN FULL FOR SERVICES

paying in full for services, for the only "cure," bringing the balance to
zero, could loosen up
New Eroticisms
untouched by obscenities, which is good for building confidence.

This important realization about being regularly overwhelmed by
Pounding Sensualities
invites comparison to a fool and a wiseman wearing hats with the same
brim, a narrative which might open up a possible zone of
Untapped Eroticisms.

An old saying sheds light on the outstanding balance, which might involve
Healthy Appetites.

> punctual for an appointment
> by becoming engaged in a dose
> of sensuality, one of the compass points.

Choosing to have a professional to talk it over with, in a clean room,
could disengage
New Possibilities
such as men drinking foamy beer early in the building and loosening up,
although their bowels are in trouble, is good for you.

Strongly wanted to hear mostly dirty talk, which might involve arriving
late due to bad timing to restore thought processes to
Steady Equilibria.

an unconscious motivation behind actions said the filthiest things, very
graphic which restored the underlying motives to
Horizontal Equilibria.

Carolyn Lei-lanilau

XIANDAI: MODERNITY

The small breast girls come to the river
to wash their *qi pao*
where jealous others gossip

"There she goes again"

"Takes off her blouse"

"Shameful slut"

"Raped one, too bad you live"

Squeezing their own wobbly thighs
the men and boys don't care:

They stare at the soft faces
nimble hands and quick toes.

Short breasts are good
and easy to live with

Gerald Locklin

AT THE SCORE

i'm enjoying the film and
already phrasing in my mind how
i may best convey to my classes the
extent to which a hidden protagonist
is the city of montreal myself,

when i realize for the first time how
close i am to retirement,
at which point,
for the first time in over forty years,
i will not have any captive class with
whom to share my thoughts, as i have
done so freely, comprehensively, and
gratefully since my first year as a
teaching assistant in 1961, having,
from then back to the age of four,
shared them with my teachers and
my classmates.

and i am terrified that,
deprived of that forum,
i will cease to bother thinking at all.

Fred Moramarco

MY SHOES

When do my shoes become MY shoes?
Not when they're first bought,
fresh and leathery out of the box,
the new shoe smell, mahogany and plums, still with them,
as I unwrap the paper that tucks them in.
And not the first time I slip them on,
sliding toes, instep, arch, and heel
into their deep, inviting tunnel of warmth.
It takes a while before I notice
a pair of MY shoes, sticking out from under my bed,
unmistakably mine, the leather creased and bruised,
the folds and scuffs witnesses to my daily travails,
walking here and there, going with me everywhere.

Everywhere people are buried with shoes on,
the skin of another animal gloving their feet,
decaying with them, though more slowly,
in their coffined berths, where skeletons with shoes
lie beneath the earth, lingering long after the life
those shoes carried from one place to another
in this known world is as empty as MY shoes are,
lying there, still and unassuming, under my bed,
without me in them, but clearly MY shoes,
and no one else's, my signature, my fingerprint,
my sheaths against the hard earth's jagged surface,
my companions in the inert world below.

Matt Morris

BEING & BEING DEAD

Perhaps the most
noticeable difference
is the lack of mobility. Not
only do overt motions
like lighting a cigarette
as you punch up work
or wife on your cell
phone to complain you're
running late, doing eighty
easy down the interstate
while rummaging
your stash for an apropos
CD or waving your hand
frantically at the screeching,
horn-blaring, diesel-
belching semi all at once
become impossible, but
also small,
internal movements—such
as those letting you discern
the tocsin of shattering
glass before doped-up,
burglarizing bunglers duct
tape your mouth & tie
you with anonymous blood-
stained nylons to your chair,
terrified—are done. In this
way particularly,
death distinguishes itself
from sleep. For instance,
the little girl, covers pulled
over her head, dreaming

she's a cloud while the red
house around her burns, never
wakes to the soot-smirched
face under the firefighter's
mask, who, lost
in a suicidal brown
study of smoke climbing
stairs that dramatically
drop into the paradoxes
of an Escher woodcut,
can't, coughing, reach her
or her deadhead daddy,
his mortal clump of ashes
smoldering in the embers
of his big ass recliner,
brew in one hand, righteous
doobie in the other, forever
nodding, watching
the eternal loop of *This
Is Your Life* reruns. You can't
be somewhat or temporarily
dead. Imagine your worst
nightmare, bugged-eyed, flush-
cheeked, smelly, mushy
flesh shrouded in a ratty, sadly
revealing mini when her
beastly heart suddenly revives,
wanting you to take her
to a movie & maybe
out clubbing later. Dead
is dead as an empty
barrel, minus the barrel
making its ringed impression
on your forehead, your
taunting, cursing ex's wacky
new flame fingering

your demise. You aren't
conscious of being dead, looking
back at the daffodils strewn
over your grave as you
ascend the celestial
escalator. For
having an awareness of being
dead is, ironically if not
gratefully, not dead,
but, you know, the other thing,
alive.

Elisabeth Murawski

ARMS

Even your house knows
her arms want to surround you:
paintings slide to the floor.
The piano tries to hide
under the sofa.
The aluminum siding
turns blue. There are several

accidents. Scorned,
her arms grow long
and longer
until they reach across
two counties, patriotic
monuments, the tiger

in the Potomac.
The city darkens
with her need. But you
are not afraid.
Not even when you hear her
yellow fingers snapping
in the garden
to an old song, an old song,
an old song.

You who pity horses,
in their loneliness
born without arms,
lift the needle
and the mantra stops.
Her arms shrivel back
to where they came from.

Then all is quiet
in your own back yard.
You take off your shoes
and dance.
Your holy hair flies up.

Muriel Nelson

TELLTALE

When I Was Still Dead, my son said
of the time before I was pregnant,
when the garden was eaten by bugs.

What is a bud? What is born
as a hostess gift, bundled
in yellow-green, to predators;

a sweet wish growing tall in dream,
in the upper bunk where the roof
is so thin roofing nails stick through.

A son is the story of a shadow
on the wall—the steam you can't see.
He's a float. Then he's disconnected.

He's an unbalanced load, a bang,
a start, a pound, a slammed
basketball—super-woofer—door—

floorboards of a body, or
(when I was still alive)
a body's heart.

B.Z. Niditch

A FRANK O'HARA DAY

Nowhere is night time
and laughter parallel,
if not the sidewalk
of spring sadness
and spilled beer
after a piano bar
tenders the grapevine report
about one-act charades
while watching *Criss-Cross*.
Yours is the deflowered
way up nine elevator shafts
toward bus stations
and the last cruise
on the youngest morning
of the newest night
shone through a hole
in a lace curtain
at the edge of the railway stop.

"Wasn't Yvonne DeCarlo
perfect for the part?"

Louis Phillips

JOHNNY INSKLINGER PRESUMES TO CUT IN ON FRED ASTAIRE WHILE HE IS DANCING WITH GINGER ROGERS

With flat feet & far away look,
I have little sense of rhythm
And/or Time,
Tho Time weighs upon my shoulders
To a fare-thee-well.

Is that a violin playing
Or a petunia with petals of lead?
Ah the palpable feet!
External organs of locomotion
Gallanting all over the lot,
Sennights of gallumphing rhumba/
Cha cha/cavortte obbligato.

Poetry has my two left feet on tap.
Ah! to whirl with unurgent grace,
Raise metal mercury
A quarter inch or son,
Make my quietus with bare bodice.

Dance, Fool, Dance.
My legs like furniture, Queen Anne Style,
Pedals of lead.
Down the stair, thru the ballroom,
Out to the patio,
Onto the beaded lawn frowsy with stars,
Sweet sea-lavender redolent with waltz.

O how I wish I cd dance with everything
That stains the lyrical world!

Lee Rossi

SURVIVOR

Sure, I believe in decorum. But we haven't had any rules around here
since Pa put the shotgun in his mouth, and pulled the—you know.
It was right after that that Tucker started sleeping with Belle.
Well, he'd always slept with her, but now they were "sleeping together."
That was too much for Ma. Joey the dog liked it though.
He started humping the dining room suit until there was nothing
left but kindling. Joey's a big dog, a cross between a Labrador
and a mountain range. But like I says, it didn't sit right with Ma,
her two youngest entwined every night in carnal embraces,
that's what the preacher said. Was bad enough all the older ones
was dead, or run off, or doing five to ten in the state pen.
Personally, none of it bothered me. I was still, as the poet says,
trailing clouds of glory, but when Ma stuck her head in the, you know,
and the whole house, including them 2 layabeds, blew up,
well, I was kinda left on my own. That's why I come to you
this Thanksgiving, hat in hand, hungry, but glad to be alive.

Mary Ruefle

THE LITTLE I SAW OF CUBA

She regained her sight for five days and she said
I cannot be left alone with the lettuce
I cannot be left alone with the lettuce—
the salad strewn in the salad bowl,
the bite-sized leaves and the red shreds
terrified her with tremendous color
and then she was blind again—
operation unsuccessful—
and I remember one other thing:
she traveled.
This surprised me for I could see
and I did not travel
and the contrast terrified me
while making a kind of calm sense,
especially when I was sleeping,
for I often thought of Cuba
and felt safe in the tropics,
walking among fronds with nothing to do
but watch red lizards climbing the wall.
Of course I have never been to Cuba,
but it remains a place
where I have never found it necessary
to alter my description of anything.

Mary Ruefle

INTERMITTENCE

The anxiety of spring will come
and the birds build nests
out of circular ideas.

Slender of means, sparing of words,
the rain will fall.

The sun will shine and make things certain.

These things will remain a mystery.

Next no contra from anywhere
and the air be seriously entangled.

Ravi Shankar

LANGUAGE POETRY

Yea, it was pundit debunking, sage with newness,
Meaty ruse, elaborate masquerade of unmeaning,

Stage where words pose counterpoised to signification,
Where rummy syllables string along kinks of syntax

And gum of virgules jimmies together clauses
To devise a monument of fistulous happenstance,

Subverting address for free play—
Rare vestiges pitched headlong in stochastic

Eddies, dreaming a livelong laterality,
Polygons alongside tapirs in grammar-shorn dance—

Slithered mid-speech an intention a seam
The color of politics, even the furthest minutia

Run on dollars, come what cannot until (s)pace
Breaks into half itself &

Music the bramble where bare verbs rabble,
Seeking the iota behind the bestial bars

That proves no forged lattice girds the mind
With predicates efficacious as prison searchlights—

Senses slip the faster usurps fate from syntax
How kowtow to solipsism or preset a page?

Ron Silliman

~~~

From *VOG*

          Having
pulled
   the
      t
   shirt
over
     my
head
       in
      the
         dark
      backwards
I
   descend
              the
            unlit
               stairs
              stepping
            carefully
              to
               avoid
                 the
               small
                  toys
               and
                  Lego
                        pieces
               I
               know
             are

                out
              there
                    waiting

The
    sound
    of
      rain
steady
        at
          first
        dissolves
            under
                  the
              simple
            hum
            of
          houselights
          as
            they
              go
            on

Lightning!

            Crows
        still
          in
            silhouette
          on
            the
          branches
              of
                the
                    tree
                  the

        sky
                brilliant
        flickering

Unable
upon
        waking
                to
                identify
        the
                young
                woman
                        with
        whom
                in
                        the
                dream
        I've
                just
                        made
                love

                        Great
                bug
                        chorus
                of
                night
                        more
                        audible
                                upstairs
                        than
                                down

Ron Silliman

TOWARD AN ANNIVERSARY OF A DROWNING IN THE SENSES

From *VOG*

For Dan Davidson

On the deck a sparrow hops unnoticed at the feet of the diners. Between high rises, the Kingdome peeks through, doomed palace. Think: if the coast is to the right, I'm facing south. Sunlight on a red potato. Next to games, the section on loss and grieving. Jet passes through a clear sky. Barge backlit by the setting sun. Overhead, the richest man in the world helicopters home. Overheard, the song of unseen traffic. She throws her head back before she laughs. A man with a parachute is pulled into the air like a kite. Lawn chairs tack up these highrise balconies. The cranes are orange because. Deep baritone of the container ship's horn. Will we be able to read this in the morning? Already the hush of dark on those far hills while here the sun blinds us to the mahi-mahi on the plate. She fiddles with both earrings at once. Offshore, those clouds foretell narrative. The mall at night. The cops all about the fallen man, wrists cuffed behind his shirtless back. What I want, what I want, what I really really want is to return to the body, preferably yours.

Ron Silliman

STORMING WAUMBEC MOUNTAIN
BY GOLF CART

From *VOG*

For Jackson Mac Low & Anne Tardos

Book chosen to read while you drive. Plastic spoon in my pocket when I reach for my pen. "My other language is French." Fog in the pine chaparral gives way to glare. Semi-permanent catsup spot upon your cheek. Moosebreath. Alleged chalet turns out to be rapidly declining old motel. In the distance, unseen, cars are driving over the iron grates of a metal bridge. Three layers of cloud. Lone segment of picket fence in the middle of a vast lawn, connected to nothing. Jefferson Notch. Age at which each local boy demonstrates humor vis-a-vis the name of Mount Martha. We took turns. She seemed pleased. Smoke there in those trees signals a home. Full moon on a clear night just before dawn. A hum in the barn next door even before daylight. Crow the loudest of the morning singers. Rather than build a new house, he decides in 1880 to raise the entire L-shaped structure up and to insert a new floor underneath it. Old two-piece phone set (no dialer) built into a small lamp: when you pick up the ear-piece, the light comes on. Two fields over, a man is walking toward some cows. Now the distinct call of the geese. First car of morning, walkers take warning. Even before the sun arrives, the swollen moon is reduced. Flock of something. We enter through a door in the greenhouse, then as I rise up the dark stairs to the kitchen of what I believe to be an empty house, the door opens and I'm staring into the startled face of Anne Tardos. Soil, as a verb. Hands about my mug of tea, even its warmth failing.

Rick Smith

FROM THE WREN NOTEBOOK

—After Barry Gifford

Wren did not know how to forage,
"Why don't these poets get to the point?"
she asked.
Wren went nearly crazy until
she learned to fly.

By April,
Wren was a nervous wreck.
"Why does this wind shift
so suddenly, why can't
these updrafts lay flat?"
she asked.
When the council of birds laughed as one,
she regurgitated barleycorn
and leg of violin spider.

Swallows peal off from the front
of the formation to draft at
the back.
Air passes through Wren
without a trace.
"Are we there yet?"
she asks.

Alan Sondheim

THE CONTINUITY GIRL

The continuity girl asserts the fundamental forces of the world. She writes 5; then 5/under erasure; she writes 4; she exhausts the series. She adds the cosmological constant, planck's constant; she erases them; she includes them; she erases them. The slate is a mess. The slate is unreadable. The slate mimics the world. The slate becomes the world. She continues to write. She is wearing a baggy sweater and carrying a Polaroid camera. She carries a great number of accessories: tripod, telephoto, wide-angle, scanning-transmission electron microscope, interferometer, neutron telescope. There are a continuous number of scenes; she numbers them according to the continuum. It is not so difficult to describe the actors; they are also continuous, and the transformation of props and objects occurs according to aristotelian logic and fluid morphology. Only certain quantum leaps give her trouble, but these radical discontinuities also permit discontinuities within or across scenes, and need not be annotated. For the rest, everything appears relatively differentiable. The slate is a mess. The slate is a continuous mess.

Alan Sondheim

TAKE OF THE CONTINUITY GIRL

The continuity girl wears a big baggy sweater and carries a clipboard and Polaroid camera. She walks among the naked actors and actress and takes notes, whose hand is where, which face is turned towards—and which away from—the camera. This is amazing. whose finger has a torn nail—whose breasts already damp—the degree of nipple erection (easy here)—all of this is carefully noted by the continuity girl. There is sweat running from a shoulder. The terrorist has his knife to a neck from the left—no, from the right—side; "R" appears almost by command on the continuity chart. Is this the numbered scene, the only scene—the continuity girl knows, takes everything into account. She writes "Alan is gagged tightly, he is having trouble breathing. If he suffocates, this will be the only take." She writes "n/g" as the gag is loosened. Azure has been shaved, head to toe; Azure is constantly shuddering. The continuity girl writes "Azure moves—lock structure in edit—there is no room for error—there is nothing but error." The continuity girl notes the bruises and bites on four, on five, breasts. She notes, "Day 3." She notes, "This is the second day." It is the goal of the continuity girl to make sure the world is whole, to make sure it remains contained, coherent, logical beneath the chaos the rest of us take for granted.

Alan Sondheim

UNIT MO

The continuity girl is nervous. She has dreamed of blood. The set has many actors. She is sure about her dream. She says "You are deranged." She says "This is a film not to be made." She says to the director "There are no actors." She says to the director "I will be your actress." She says to the director "Do with me what you will." She annotates all continuity. She says "There is no director." She says "I am the director." She says "I am sure of it.":The continuity girl wears her baggy sweater. She removes her sweater. She removes her shirt. She removes her bra. She removes her pants. She removes her panties. She removes her tampon. She removes her stopwatch. She puts down her continuity pad. She puts down the script. She picks up the script. "I will be the star of this and every other film." The day is night. Her shaved hair is long. Her brown eyes are blue. Her perfect teeth are crooked. Her heavy legs are thin. Her small breasts are large. America harbors terrorists in many suburban tracts. They are set to move against Afghanistan their mortal enemy. Afghanistan is crossroads of empire. Fundamentalists stream across oceans. Afghanistan is mortally wounded. The script is soaked in blood. The continuity girl climbs a tree. The continuity girl wraps up. She has observed the continuity girl. Against her will she has participated in the film. There are broken costume changes. The sky is another weather. Her mood is broken. She did give herself to herself. She did wound herself from the convenient tree. She did pick up the script from the ground. She did put it inside of herself. She did read of it through her period the blood. She did note the crevice of blood across the page. She did note the word "supple""ment" cut between one stroke and another. :odin-theme:script boy

The continuity girl wraps up. She has observed the continuity girl. Against her will she has participated in the film. There are broken costume changes. The sky is another weather. Her mood is broken. She did give herself to herself. She did wound herself from the convenient tree. She did pick up the script from the ground. She did put it inside of herself. She did read of it through her period the blood. She did note the crevice of blood across the page. She did note the word "supple""ment" cut between one stroke and another. Replace the continuity girl is nervous. She has dreamed of blood. The set has many actors. She is sure about her dream. She says "You are deranged." She says "This is a film not to be made." She says to the director "There are no actors." She says to the director "I will be your actress." She says to the director "Do with me what you will." She annotates all continuity. She says "There is no director." She says "I am the director." She says "I am sure of it." She is naked-woman. The film is War-Time Fuck. The film is The Truth About Angels. The film is Apocalypse Now. The film is Biograph Continuity Girl. The film is Mistake of the Century. The film is Miss Take.

Alan Sondheim

BIOGRAPH CONTINUITY GIRL

who is the continuity girl. she writes and underlines these words; she checks spelling and stylistic consistency. in the world, she writes, she makes certain that day is day, night is night; that if day for night, then not night for day; if night for day, then not day for night. she wears careful glasses, is twenty-three years old, and a graduate of ucla's motion picture / television department. she has been an extra in several post-blair-witch-project student films, shot in will rogers state park. she is originally from portland, maine. she studied with leslie thornton in brown university's modern culture and media department for her undergraduate work. it was only later that she decided to remain on the periphery of cinema, closely observing everything around her. the film was secondary, she writes, to the continuous reiteration of the real. she thinks she is a machine. she thinks she is the perfect eye. she thinks she is the inconceivable eye. i am the continuity girl, she writes, who am i.

who is the continuity girl. she writes and underlines these words; she is killing everything. everything is destroyed and mutilated. what damage have you done; she... a soldier rapes me. i rape a soldier. i am terror. i am terror of the real. i make certain that day is day, night is night; that if day for night, then what is mine, who is the continuity girl. she writes and underlines these words: SHE IS YOURS. SHE IS YOUR BIOTERRORISM HERE. i dream of the naked dead-man, she writes. i am hungry. i make things.

she is in the armor. she writes, i owe everything to leslie thornton and john malkovich. she writes, i will be naked all the time. she takes off her baggy sweater. she writes, i am of the real. n/g. i am the real. i am film. armies film me. i will write their names. the glass is on the right-hand side. it is cloudy out and 9 o'clock in the early night. she writes, people are dying. she writes, people are staring at me.

i am happy.

she makes certain that day is day, night is night; that if day for night, then:checks spelling and stylistic consistency. in the world, she writes, she:who is the continuity girl. she writes and underlines these words; she:thinks she is a machine. she thinks she is the perfect eye. she thinks she :careful glasses, is twenty-three years old, and a graduate of ucla.

Denise L. Stevens

SEPTEMBER CATALOGUE

I want and then don't want. Pale Green or Sprig, Plum
or Merlot. Waffled, quilted, flanneled, satined, feathered.
By page 63, I need a Primaloft hypoallergenic body pillow,
one of twelve perfect mattress pads, a few Westport Chenille
Decorator Throws. I nap and napping dream of golden
Garden Trellis shower curtains. The paperbacks snooze
in their jackets, the news hides under chairs. The right questions
are never answered: When did Haze become the color of silk?
Of fresh cut flower soaps? Oh, Buttercream, oh, sweet, scalloped
pumpkin forest, end of summer chaise, how many geese are weeping
through your lovely leaves?

Denise L. Stevens

f-STOP

the butterknife for emphasis
flings its everywhere
little frogponds of
little firestorms
(my father misspeaks: I wasn't
fabliau   field   flower
under the influence
((which function key finds me
flashy   fallow
all bilabial fricatives have
help)) frustration
meaning
though they be not
born under those damn conifers)
ekphrasis?   film speed?
phonemes
specifically: D's follies
[the boning knife enters
stage left]
fontanel   fraternal
fronds I said
from a palmist's tree
sorry
I grew up thinking fuck
a fine word
not for sex but
in *fuchsia flagrante*
rhetorical finger-pointing
fourchette   fountain
fortune's daughter

[that's a lovely forgetfulness
you've fermented there
sir may I have a fifth?]
folie a deux a trois
I am not proud of it
fuss or fizzle mister
there is no far
though the feng shui master free
the falconer and the chi

Terese Svoboda

NIPPLE

A smaller dollop of people
and we could pass.
But even arms akimbo, no.
Instead, we throw our heads clear

and there's the moon.
You reach up and cup it.
People push past us—they do, they do—
and we could be leaves

filled and lifted
among them
except the light is
what lifts us,

moon enough for everyone.
But only you
brushed it,
so hard and full.

Paula Szuchman

THE TERMS

We did it
five times a week,
then three,
then one.
I wouldn't go below
one.
We wouldn't
burn out
on my watch.
We worked back
up to three.
We held steady.
I bought electric toys
and feathers.
Once, we did it
in the movie theater.
That was cool.
Another time underneath
the stair
where we kept
our trunk of winter clothes.
The seasons changed.
In the park,
a million
squirrels pillaging the fields,
a million acorns,
one for each.

James Tate

ELEGY FOR SPOOKY

My dog, Spooky, would bring me the paper
in the morning. Then he would sit at the kitchen
table and watch me read it. When I was finished,
he would take it to the trashcan and drop it in.
Once, when I was raking leaves in the front yard,
a man jumped out of a tree and attacked me. Spooky
came running and immediately pinned the man to the
ground with a firm grip on his neck. In gratitude,
I took Spooky to his favorite restaurant in town
and bought him a T-bone steak. I talked to Spooky
all through dinner, just as I would anyone, and
he would nod and whimper. He understood every word
I said. One day we were walking in the country,
and suddenly we were surrounded by a pack of wolves.
I thought that was the end of us both. I was trembling
and praying and Spooky was snarling as if he meant it.
The wolves narrowed their circle, hissing. Spooky
started telling them wolf jokes, which at first
they didn't understand. But then one of them started
to laugh, then another, until the whole pack of
them was howling with amusement. I walked around
patting them on their heads and giving them dog
biscuits, which, of course, they had never had before.
I think Spooky just made those jokes up on the spot.
That night we drank champagne and feasted, grateful
to be alive. "Spooky," I said, "Spooky, Spooky."

James Tate

JULES TO THE RESCUE

Jules said he would come over and see if
he could fix my stereo. It had not been working
in months, and I had really missed listening to
music. When he arrived, he was all business.
He went right to work. He pulled out all the
wires. "I don't know what you've done here, Mac,
but this is a mess," he said. I just stood back
and watched him. He seemed disgusted, and I
didn't know what to say. "Somebody's tried to
sabotage this whole system," he said. "Do you
have any rye bread?" "I do," I said. "How much
do you need?" "Three slices ought to do it," he
said. I brought them to him and he went on working.
A while later he asked me for a couple of golf balls.
He was working furiously. "How's it going?" I asked.
"We're getting there," he said. "Could you get me
some toothpaste and maybe some pinto beans?" "No
problem," I said. A little scratchy stuff was
beginning to come out of the speakers. Jules was
good. I knew he could help me, if he could find
the time. "One last thing, Mac. Do you think
you could find some Queen Anne's lace in the back-
yard?" "I'll try," I said. I looked and looked
and finally I found just a little bit. "That should
be enough," he said. And he went on working for
another half-hour. Then, lo and behold, glorious
music started pouring from the speakers, crisp
and clear as never before. "Thank you, Jules,"
I said, "I thank you from the bottom of my heart.
"Hey, you got to have music. But that's a very
strange system you have there. It's almost human,
it's heading that way. You should keep an eye
on it, and call me if anything funny happens. Okay?"

James Tate

DOPPELGANGER

A man gave me a funny look, so I gave him
a funny look back. Then he gave me another funny
look, and I returned it. "Is something bothering
you?" he said. "Yeah," I said, "we both keep getting
these funny looks on our faces." "Well, I'll stop
if you will," he said. "I'm willing to try," I said.
Just as he was about to turn away, I shot him this
really screwy look. "I saw that," he said. "That
one was an accident," I said. "I didn't even know
I had it in me. I was thinking about something else."
"Nonetheless," he said, "it came out and it was aimed
at me." "I'll turn and run away and that will be
the end of that," I said. "But where would you go?
You might scare people. I, at least, am getting
used to you and your horrible faces," he said.
"But you started all this, remember? I was just
out for a stroll. I needed some air. My eyes were
fuzzy. My nose itched," I said. "The same could
be said of me," he said. "And how do you feel now?"
I inquired. "Much better. I can see perfectly well,"
he replied. "Yes, it seems we've had a curative
effect on one another, after all," I said. And now
that my eyes were clearing, I could see that he was
nothing more than a reflection of myself in a store-
front window. I made my fiercest grimace, bowed
politely, and walked away, promising to return.

Judith Taylor

COURT JESTER

Danny Kaye AKA David Kaminski looked
Jewish so Sam Goldwyn, who thought

the goyim preferred looking at their own
on the big screen, made him dye his dark hair

and eyebrows reddish blonde. I love Danny's
pompadour. I admit I had a crush on him

when young. My father took me to see
The Court Jester, one of the few times

I can remember the two of us having fun. Oh
that Danny boy—his pirouettes and entrechats,

his racy-spacey tongue sputtering fractured French,
Italian, German. In jester tights his long slim legs

rested in third or fourth position, the few
seconds he wasn't in motion. Abracadabra!

Watch grace dissolve into campy gawkiness.
When the jester's knighted so he can be killed

in joust by burly Sir Griswold, the hours-long
ceremony has to be sped up—five minutes is all

it takes. Danny's marched to and fro, right and left,
between rows of ironclad solders. His armor's

magnetized: he keeps banging into everyone.
He's held up, shuffling, between the strutting

guys, his knees and feet sticking out at right angles,
a plie in air. I laughed so hard I started coughing.

Daddy loved to point out each famous face
who was one of us: Kirk Douglas, Tony Curtis.

Danny, our blonde fool, tender, silly, our Jew.
Love scenes with Glenis Johns had no chemistry.

I didn't know from gay or bisexual then (hey,
I didn't even know about sex!) and if Daddy

had suspected he'd have made fun of him and
we wouldn't have gone. Dad reached for my hand

as we walked home from the theater.
I let him hold it.

Elaine Terranova

MINT

Already, we'd be driving past
those trees, that part of the forest.
Even briefly, it refreshed you.
It was like mint in August
though that sting would be gone
with summer. The ground
tarnishing first, and soon the leaves.
I thought then, men don't stop.
They want so much to get on.
What we said, incidental
yet hammered into the mind.
Talk like a magnet, so it draws you
together or away. We made a line
around that part of the forest,
the exact shape of our attention.
Even after, I remember
how it was taken up and moved
along with us, into the dim
living room. Each holding a glass,
ice colliding in water. A tiny
mirrored sun caught in the trees.
The same sadness that darkened
our features. Later, bed
without making love, without
the chance of a reprieve.

Leslie Ullman

THE OTHER LIFE

Someone is drifting below the window
murmuring, *I'm happy*, astonished,
this evening of stripped trees
and empty benches, of leaves

crackling like old skins underfoot,
every bush and flower dismantled
for winter, the street musicians gone.
Happy. The word unfurls, a rose

in the bowl of itself,
its petals lending hue and weight
to other words that have no irony,
no record of significant

battles, no negotiable coinage
in the realm of the concrete—
gossamer, sunburst, soul—
who of us would turn

from the window, the parted
blindness of curtains, if such a word
might breathe something silky, shot with dawn,
another life to wrap around the shoulders?

Each of us, it seems, is shadowed by a slow-
moving planet that crests the horizon
just as we slip into this world, this life
of ignorance and intention—

Pluto with its treads and blades
that plow things apart and leave them
ready for seed; Neptune, lord
of poetry and brooding

and affairs that come to no good;
Saturn, tireless teacher who
strews the way with boulders, chasms,
a crosshatch of winds, the selves

we think we've outgrown
waiting to be picked up and carried. . .
Lucky person down there, whose happiness
is the moon just rising, full for a time

even though its light is borrowed and bemused—
moon bright enough to cast shadows—
who of us wouldn't try for just one
dance in the broken darkness?

Charles Harper Webb

THE SECRET OF WYATT EARP

He was a brave man, but terrified to sneeze.
"It's like my soul sprays out," he told his wife.
"I feel spent afterwards—spent and afraid."

His wife kissed him. "Oh Wyatt," she teased,
but quashed an urge to blow her nose.
He had hay fever before the OK Corral,

and spent the whole day sneezing, right up to the fight.
"I almost didn't go," he said. "I felt so weak.
But that just made me meaner when the guns came out."

I read this in a book by Wyatt's great-grandson,
a bald electrician of average height
who turned up in my class, "Becoming a New Man."

He wore a suit with a red handkerchief that sulked
in his breast pocket like an eel. He sniffed
a lot and rubbed his nose, but never sneezed.

I was young then, searching for secrets.
I wanted to believe in someone—even Wyatt Earp—
to overcome my fears and make a name.

Instead, I started mega-dosing antihistamines,
spending my spare time avoiding drafts.
I'm old now. No one's heard of me.

Susan Wheeler

WAIT!

There are too many people in my lobby,
          tripping my alarm.

I waited all day for you, you are not in the
          worksheets, you are not among them.

Are they waiting for their wages? Bobbing
          their headphones like Trix in milk.

The guard's slipped a mickey and now squalls
          gather at my elevators.

You said you would be there, did I mis-hear
          his translation?

They leave their headphones on when they enter,
          they chitchat at me.

I who have slight currency in this, O you
          who are vinegar on his tongue.

Eve Wood

HUNTER GREEN

The color is misnamed.
Never would green take up the rifle
and traipse into the forest
as though to slaughter itself everywhere—
trees, bushes, the serpentine necks of vines
extending savagely around the dark branches.
Never would green dishonor its truest nature,
while red had always been a traitor,
a practitioner of fecklessness and greed,
watching as green hid deep inside its own saturation,
refusing to come forward.
I've lived my life on a burning foundation;
an onslaught of yellows and reds
determine my days,
so when I saw him standing in that green sweater
like an invitation to trust
all that is calm and at peace around me,
I felt I had been given permission
to die, to lie down with my imagination
and nothing more, submit finally to the augury
of the sparrow's flight,
making its way from the slim, feminine arms of the birch tree
to the barrel-chested oak.

Renate Wood

PURGATORY, ETC.

It happens that I'm waiting in line
at the post office or some cash register and suddenly
find myself staring down long rows of beet greens
in a landscape of morning mist hanging low in hulks
like slaughtered sheep. Between the fields
I'm standing inside a crowded streetcar, one hand
holding on to a leather loop hanging from the lit ceiling
along with other loops and hands stretched up
above a crowd of bodies pressed against each other
in raincoats, work shirts, suits next to the rows of bodies
seated along still darkened windows, a dense
human cargo lost among miles of sugar beets,
while in the distance a single tractor moves back and forth
mechanically like a clock's pendulum. Crows
punctuate the distant hum. From where they caw
we must look like the lantern a farmer left for the new milk truck
by the turn-off. The streetcar is stopped.
Its doors do not open. What are we waiting for?
God is nowhere to be seen, nor is the milkman—
who could find anyone out in this curdled air?
We're waiting for the streetcar from the city, lit up like Santa Lucia,
to come out through the suburbs and into the lowland mist.
No place is as lonely as the split track of a siding
far from the city, dazzling with hundreds of streetcars,
lamps along the avenues, and people moving freely
across the bridge and through the station doors.
We're waiting, and we're weary although it is
just after dawn in the beet fields, watching for the conductor
to drop his cigarette and lean out of the window
to hand a brightly colored token to the conductor of the streetcar
from the city and for the cars to pass each other, heading
in opposite directions back onto the single track.

Once waiting for a friend years ago after school, I sat
feeding the ducks by the river, where the water was
green like the fields but continually flowing. Wherever
it passed, it seemed to be just arriving; the ducks
knew that and kept on stretching their downy necks
into my hand so that I soon forgot that I was waiting and came to
suddenly, as all the steamers and barges began blowing their horns.
You wouldn't believe the racket, it could have reached
as far as the beet fields where I've spent half my life,
and now when I think of the man out there on the tractor,
he might have paused to listen and chew on bread
soaked in molasses, tasting the sweetness
that lay hidden in all those fields and, who knows,
also in us, and the conductor could have tossed his token
in a wide arc into the air, for then we were no longer waiting,
but looking at each other, breathing a long, deep sigh, as if
it were here, at this moment, we had meant to arrive.

Gail Wronsky

MY CHILDHOOD, IF IT HAD TAKEN PLACE IN AN ACTUAL DESERT

We used to think   that giants lived
          in the rock wells next to Ocotillo. We
     used to say   that red-tailed hawks turned
               into creosote bushes when they died,
the way   the Cloud People   of
Los
          Coyotes Indian Reservation became
          mariposa lilies. We
thought that   chuparosa scraped its
          bony fingers across the dry white desert
sky   just to make children
     unhappy.

We said, "What is imperfect   is best," and
          believed it,
just as we believed that the rattle of boulders repeated
               the oozing of wet clay
but in a different   dialect.   At the creekbed,
     where poisonous mushrooms grew, we sang
          only the truest poems—

     Lizard-tongue, lizard-tongue:
     Spit us some rain.

     Our parents have married;
     Life is insane.

Gail Wronsky

ELEGY FROM A NIGHTINGALE'S POINT OF VIEW

Jug jug twit twit tereu

He came as if in exile to a docile
west, having long ago
forgiven his exes who
univocally seemed to be at
their wits' ends when not
having premonitions about him.

He seemed too
disorganized for the Murphy bed
in the Peter Pan apartments
on Second South where, at 47, he
committed himself to never
reaching adulthood. Where he
fancied his collections of fine pens and
razors. Where on occasion he'd
artfully shave a woman's leg
then paint her biggest toenail
obsidian, blowing on it till it was
as hard as glass. Then he'd measure out
a coffee spoon of cocaine
powder over the tip of it, and
up across the arch of her
foot, sometimes trailing it off
all the way to her knee cap. You'd
have to lie perfectly
still while he scraped toward your
middle with his straw,
afterwards fastidiously
licking with his king-of-cat's
tongue just those places where
the coke had been.

He wanted to be like the man in the
Magritte painting whose head
was only sky—absolved of all of it and
all-absolving—

but maybe he wasn't able to
forgive the rapist of Philomel.
And maybe behind the fleshy
mask of his face was the
smooth face of a
newer mask. Maybe he
did eat that much
speed. Maybe in some book a
picture of a train had
spoken to him, saying:
Take me to the city built
entirely by slaves of love,
and so he'd taken it (the picture)
somewhere, having wanted to see for
himself a city built by
sad-eyed casanovas like him.
Maybe dying was
a consequence of his
rejecting certain commonplaces
widely proliferated in this time,
the one perhaps which
claims a poet's life,
well, matters . . . I
do think it was all
let go by him finally: the
girls with no tongues who
took his poetry workshops, the
flies around the soda cans,
the song
96 Tears sung by that

LA punk band (as if
by a fly, the 96
tears coming out of its 96
multi-prismed eyes . . .),
the migrant workers'
banda music, the problem in
Utah of getting a
martini dry. *I'll do*
anything for you, he whimpered to
Bank of America in
the middle of the night once, pounding his
hand against an impenetrable
drive-through window drawer until
he shattered a bone: *just let me have a*
little of my own money . . . If the
bank had been a
woman, it would've
given him what he
wanted. In
fact, a woman I
know came
forward with some
cash that night and
he left town with her,
looking from behind as if a
plump fetus were
pushing its head down through his
shirt collar, and I
never saw him again. Maybe
it was his
tongue on my kneecap.
Maybe his baby-face, or his
rough beard or the
wind coming in freezing from
the Uintas. Maybe the
way he assumed we'd all been

forced to
do things that were,
in some other life, unthinkable, and
because of that, we were all both
guilty (of the knowledge)
and of the deeds,
whatever they were, and also
(just because, without
a need for explanation) just as
innocent as
morning. Always starting with
pure emptiness and
forgetting our alibis. Some songs were
prettier, he'd said, *despite*
the rudeness of our bringing them.
Maybe that was wisdom. Maybe it was
nothing but a kind of
genius for seduction. At
any rate, the time he
dipped a razor edge
into the artery behind my
knee and
blood shot back, staining his face, I
forgave him, almost instantly—so
difficult to see a person
wreathed like that—
and starting to weep. Or laugh. You know,
there was no stopping it.

Contributors

RONALD ALEXANDER's poems and stories have appeared in many journals. His novel, *The Final Audit*, was recently published by Hollyridge Press. He lives in Venice, California where he is at work on an historical novel set in a TB sanitorium in Indiana in the 1930's.

WILLIAM ALLEGREZZA's poetry has been published in small magazines in several countries. Recently, his chapbook *Lingo* was published by subontic press. In his spare time, he edits *Moria* (www.moriapoetry.com), a poetry e-zine.

BARRY BALLARD's sonnets have most recently appeared in *Smartish Pace*, *Rosebud*, *The Florida Rview* and *Quarterly West*. Recipient of the "Explorations Award for Literature" from the University of Alaska and the "Boswell Poetry Prize" from Texas Christian University, he has also published two prize winning collections: *Green Tombs to Jupiter* (Snail's Pace Press Poetry Prize, NY) and *A Time to Reinvent* (Creative Ash Press Poetry Prize, PA). He writes from Burleson, Texas.

JIM BARNES' new book of poetry is *On A Wing Of The Sun* (University of Illinois Press, 2001). At Truman State University he edits *The Chariton Review* and is Writer-in-Residence and Professor of Comparative Literature. He has held two Camargo Foundation Fellowships, an NEA, a Fulbright to Switzerland, a Schloss Solitude Fellowship, among others.

AARON BELZ is a graduate of NYU, presently working on a Ph.D. in English at Saint Louis University. He has published poetry in *Fence*, *Exquisite Corpse*, *Gulf Coast*, *Jacket*, with work forthcoming in *March Hares: the Best Poems from Fine Madness 1982-2002*.

BILL BERKSON is a poet, art critic and professor of Liberal Arts at the San Francisco Art Institute. His most recent books are: *Fugue State*, *25 Grand View*, and a collection of his early-'60s collaborations with Frank O'Hara, *Hymns of St. Bridget & Other Writings*.

RICK BURSKY lives in Los Angeles. His work has appeared in many journals including *Harvard Review*, *Epoch*, *Verse*, *Quarterly West*, *Poem*, *Shenandoah* and *Black Warrior Review*.

JUSTIN ISRAEL CAIN flirts with the Gatha of Impermanence. MFA from Vermont College. Voted most likely to.

KILLARNEY CLARY is the author of *By Common Salt* (Oberlin College Press) and *Who Whispered Near Me* (Farrar, Straus & Giroux). Her third collection of poems, *Potential Stranger*, will be published in Spring of 2003 by the University of Chicago Press.

CATHY COLMAN is the author of *Borrowed Dress* which won the Felix Pollock Prize in poetry.

PATRICIA CORBUS' poems have appeared in numerous journals, including *Green Mountains Review, Folio, Antigonish Review*, the *Wallace Stevens Journal, Greensboro Review, South Carolina Review, Cream City Review, Paris Review, Antioch Review, Georgia Review, Iconoclast, Cincinnati Poetry Review*, and *Kestrel*.

STEPHEN COREY has published nine collections of poems, most recently *Greatest Hits,1980-2000* (Pudding House Publications, 2000), *Mortal Fathers and Daughters* (Palanquin Press, 1999), and *All These Lands You Call One Country* (University of Missouri Press, 1992). Individually, his poems, essays, and reviews have appeared in numerous periodicals and anthologies. With Warren Slesinger he co-edited *Spreading The Word: Editors On Poetry* (The Bench Press, 2001). Corey is associate editor of *The Georgia Review*, with which he has worked since 1983.

CATHERINE DALY is a poet and member of the National Book Critics Circle. Her collection, *Locket*, is due in 2003 from Tupelo Press. Another manuscript is a finalist in the National Poetry Series.

STUART DISCHELL is the author of *Good Hope Road* (Viking, 1993), a National Poetry Series Selection, *Evenings & Avenues* (Penguin, 1996), and *Dig Safe* forthcoming from Penguin in 2003. His poems have appeared in many magazines, including, *The Kenyon Review, Partisan Review, Ploughshares, The New Republic, and Slate*. He teaches in the Master of Fine Arts Program in Creative Writing at the University of North Carolina at Greensboro and in the Program for Writers at Warren Wilson.

PATRICK DONNELLY is an Associate Editor at Four Way Books, an independent literary press in New York City (http://www.fourwaybooks.com). He is in the MFA Program in Poetry at Warren Wilson College. His writing has appeared or is forthcoming in *The Virginia Quarterly Review, The Marlboro Review, Quarterly West, Beloit Poetry Journal*, and *Ploughshares*.

MARK DuCHARME's books of poetry include *Cosmopolitan Tremble* (Pavement Saw Press, 2002) and *Anon* (with Anselm Hollo, Laura Wright, Patrick Pritchett & Jane Dalrymple-Hollo: Potato Clock Editions, 2001). Recent or forthcoming magazine appearances include *Antennae, Combo, Conundrum, Canwehaveourballback, For Immediate Release* and *Ur-Vox*. He lives in Boulder, Colorado with his wife and daughter.

KARI EDWARDS' book *post/(pink)* was published by Scarlet Press in 2000. kari's work can also be found in *Blood and Tears* (an anthology of poetry on Matthew Sheppard) from Painted Leaf Press, *The International Journal of Sexuality and Gender Studies, Bombay Gin,* and *Fracture*. kari has exhibited art work throughout the United States and is an adjunct instructor at University of Colorado—Boulder, and Naropa University, teaching Gender Studies, Creative Writing and Women's literature.

KATE FETHERSTON is a writer and psychotherapist living in Vermont. She is a student in the MFA Program at Vermont College.

ZACK FINCH lives again in Asheville, NC, where he is a student in Warren Wilson's MFA Program for Writers.

KEVIN S. FITZGERALD has had work appear in *Vert, Antenym, Prosodia* and *Vapor/Strains*. Work of his is forthcoming in *Rain Taxi* and *sidereality*. After a few years in New York City, he now works as an editor in Baltimore.

CHRIS FORHAN's work has been published recently in *Poetry, Parnassus, New England Review,* and *Ploughshares*. His book *Forgive Us Our Happiness*, winner of the Bakeless Poetry Prize, was published in 1999 by University Press of New England, and a long poem, "*x*," was published last year by Floating Bridge Press.

RICHARD P. GABRIEL is a poet, essayist, and computer scientist. His most recent book is *Writers' Workshops and the Work of Making Things*.

RICHARD GARCIA is the author of *The Flying Garcias* (University of Pittsburgh Press) and *Rancho Notorious* (BOA Editions). His poems have recently appeared in *Mid-American Review, The Colorado Review,* and the anthology *Urban Nature*, published by Milkweed Press. He is poet-in-residence at Children's Hospital in Los Angeles, assisted by a series of grants from the California Arts Council and the Johnny Mercer Foundation.

J.F. GARMON's poems have appeared in *Ploughshares, Prairie Schooner, Southern Poetry Review, Southern Humanities Review,* and other journals. He is president of Vista Community College in Berkeley, California.

ERIC GELSINGER was born in Buffalo, New York, 1977 and sometimes lives in New York. Eventually graduated first in History at the University of Buffalo and informally studied the whole time with Robert Creeley. Also studied at Oxford and lived in Xela, Guatemala, where he might be right now. Loves young poets: Edmund Berrigan, Alexander Stessin, Amerst Tigers love.

REGINALD GIBBONS has published seven books of poems, the most recent of which is *It's Time*, which has just been published by Lousiana State University Press. He has also published short stories and a novel, *Sweetbitter*. His version of Euripides' *Bakkhai*, translated with Charles Segal, was published in 2001 by Oxford University Press; his translation of Sophokles' *Antigone*, also with Charles Segal, is forthcoming from Oxford University Press.

JOY GLADDING's book *Stonecrop* won the Yale Younger Poets Prize. She teaches in the Vermont College MFA program, and translates French for a living.

ELTON GLASER edits the Akron Series in Poetry. With William Greenway, he co-edited *I Have My Own Song for It: Modern Poems of Ohio* (The University of Akron Press, 2002). His fifth book of poems, *Pelican Tracks,* won the Crab Orchard Award and will be published by Southern Illinois University Press in 2003.

RACHEL HADAS teaches English at the Newark campus of Rutgers University. She is the author of more than a dozen books of poetry, essays, and translations, most recently *Indelible* (Wesleyan University Press, 2001).

SHAUNA HANNIBAL lives in Cincinnati. Her work has appeared or is forth–coming in *Spinning Jenny* and *jubilat*.

MATT HART co-founded and co-edits *Forklift Ohio: A Journal of Poetry, Cooking & Light Industrial Safety*. His work has appeared *Conduit, Ploughshares*, *River City*, and *Spinning Jenny*. He lives in Cincinnati Ohio.

DIANNA HENNING has published in: *Fugue*; *Asheville Poetry Review*; *The Spoon River Poetry Review*, *The Red Rock Review*, *The Louisville Review*, *Crazyhorse* and *The California Quarterly*. She is a California Arts Council grant recipient and is an artist in residence at Diamond View School in Susanville, California.

TERRANCE HAYES is the author of *Hip Logic* and *Muscular Music*. He lives and teaches in Pittsburgh, PA.

DAVID HESS attended Brown University and lives in Las Vegas. Essays and reviews have appeared in *Mungo vs. Ranger, Jacket, Quid, Skanky Possum, Readme* and *Flashpoint*. A chapbook, *Cage Dances*, was published by Skanky Possum Press in 2001.

GEORGE HIGGINS is an Assistant Public Defender in Alameda County, California. He graduated from the University of Michigan Law School, and has an MFA from Warren Wilson College. His work has been published in *Squaw Review*, with poems forthcoming in *Pleiades*.

JONATHAN HOLDEN is a University Distinguished Professor of English and Poet-in-Residence at Kansas State University in Manhattan, Kansas. His latest book is *Knowing: New and Selected Poems* (University of Arkansas Press, 2000). His collection *America Frankly* is currently looking for a publisher.

ROY JACOBSTEIN's collection, *Ripe*, received the 2002 Felix Pollak Prize from the University of Wisconsin Press. Several of his poems that appeared the past year in *The Threepenny Review, The Gettysburg Review, Parnassus*, and *Poetry Daily* were nominated for a Pushcart Prize. He is a public health physician who works internationally in women's reproductive health.

MARK JARMAN's latest collection of poetry is *Unholy Sonnets*. His previous collection, *Questions for Ecclesiastes*, won the Lenore Marshall Poetry Prize for 1998. He is co-editor of *Rebel Angels: 25 Poets of the New Formalism* and co-author of *The Reaper Essays*. He is the author of two books of essays on poetry: *The Secret of Poetry*, from Story Line Press, and *Body and Soul: Essays on Poetry* from the University of Michigan's Poets on Poetry Series. He teaches at Vanderbilt University.

HALVARD JOHNSON has published four collections of poetry: *Transparencies and Projections, The Dance of the Red Swan, Eclipse*, and *Winter Journey*, all from New Rivers Press and now out of print but archived at the Contemporary American Poetry Archives <http://capa.conncoll.edu>. His poetry and fiction have appeared in *Puerto del Sol, Wisconsin Review, Mudfish, Poetry: New York, For Poetry, CrossConnect, Salt River Review, Blue Moon Review, Crania, Gulf Stream, The Florida Review* and *Synaesthetic*. Currently, he resides in New York City with his wife, the prize-winning fiction writer and painter Lynda Schor. He teaches at the Eugene Lang College of the New School University and in Newark, New Jersey, at the New Jersey Institute of Technology.

KATE KNAPP JOHNSON is the author of three collections of poetry: *When Orchids Were Flowers* (Dragon Gate, Inc.), *This Perfect Life* (Miami University Press) and, most recently, *Wind Somewhere, and Shade* (Miami University Press, 2001) which received a Gradiva Award from the National Association for the Advancement of Psychoanalysis. She teaches writing at Sarah Lawrence College and is a student at The Westchester Institute.

PETER JOHNSON's recent book of prose poems, *Miracles & Mortifications*, received the 2001 James Laughlin Award from the Academy of American Poets.

JEFFREY JULLICH is a former horoscope columnist for *Vice Magazine* and librettist for the opera *American Lit (Queer Theory): The Hawthorne-Melville Correspondence*. His poetry, criticism, and translations have most recently been published in *litvert.com* (translations of Victor Hugo's ouija-board poetry), the on-line *Electronic Poetry Review* # 3 and *Raintaxi*.

CAROLYN LEI-LANILAU is the author of *Wode Shuofa (My Way of Speaking)*, a collection of poetry which won an American Book Award in 1988 and *Ono Ono Girl's Hula*, a collection of creative non-fiction essays which won the Small Press and University Award as well as the Firecracker Award in 1998. She lectures and performs internationally while not teaching in Oakland or Hawai'i.

GERALD LOCKLIN's most recent collection of poems is *The Life Force Poems* (Water Row Press, 2002). He has published over one hundred books and chapbooks of poetry, fiction, and criticism and teaches Creative Writing and Literature at California State University, Long Beach.

FRED MORAMARCO is Editor of *Poetry International*, a poetry annual published at San Diego State University where he teaches American Literature and Creative Writing. He is co-author of *Containing Multitudes: Poetry in the United States Since 1950* and *Modern American Poetry*, and co-editor of *Men of Our Time: Male Poetry in Contemporary America*.

MATT MORRIS has most recently appeared in *Barbaric Yawp, Cape Rock, Free Lunch*, and *G.W. Review*. He also has work in the forthcoming anthology *Manthology: Poems of the Male Experience*. He holds a master's from the University of Southern Mississippi's Center for Writers at Hattiesburg.

ELISABETH MURAWSKI's book, *Moon and Mercury*, was published in 1990 by Washington Writers' Publishing House. Her chapbook, *Troubled by an Angel*, was published by Cleveland State University Poetry Center in 1997. Her poems have appeared in numerous journals and magazines, including *Hayden's*

Ferry Review, *The New Republic*, *Grand Street*, *American Poetry Review*, *Virginia Quarterly Review*, *Shenandoah*, and *Quarterly West*.

MURIEL NELSON is the author of *Part Song* (Bear Star Press, 1999). Her work has been nominated for a Pushcart Prize and has appeared in *The New Republic*, *Ploughshares*, *The Marlboro Review*, *Northwest Review*, *Drought*, and others. She is currently collaborating with a composer on a 9/11 requiem for choir, soloists, and organ.

B.Z. NIDITCH is a poet, playwright and teacher, as well as the artistic director of The Original Theatre in Boston. When not writing he enjoys playing jazz violin.

LOUIS PHILLIPS is a poet, playwright, and short-story writer. SMU Press published his collection of stories, *A Dream Where No One Dare Lives*, and Fort Schuyler Press will soon publish his new collection of stories, *The Bus to the Moon*. He has published over 35 books for children and adults.

LEE ROSSI is the author of *Beyond Rescue*. His work has appeared in the anthologies *Grand Passion, Truth & Lies That Press for Life*, and *New Los Angeles Poets*, as well as in journals such as *The Sun*, *Poetry East*, *Chelsea*, *The Wormwood Review*, *Poetry/LA* and *The Los Angeles Times*. He has also served as editor of the early 90's poetry magazine *Tsunami* and on the Organizing Committee of the Los Angeles Poetry Festival.

MARY RUEFLE's latest book is *Among the Musk Ox People* (Carnegie Mellon, 2002).

RAVI SHANKAR's work has appeared or is forthcoming in such magazines and journals as *The Paris Review*, *Gulf Coast*, *Time Out New York*, *Western Humanities Review*, *Massachusetts Review*, *Crowd*, *Lit*, *Poets & Writers*, *Mississippi Review*, and *Jacket*. He is the founding editor of the online journal of the arts, *<http://www.drunkenboat.com>* and former MC of the Night Cafe Reading Series in New York City.

RON SILLIMAN lives in Chester County, Pennsylvania, with his wife and two sons, and works as a market analyst in the computer industry. The winner of the 1985 Poetry Center Book Award for his prose poem *Paradise*, Silliman was a 1998-99 Pew Fellow in the Arts, and twice received grants from the California Arts Council as well as one from the National Endowment for the Arts. He is a 2002 fellow of the Pennsylvania Council on the Arts. His anthology *In the American Tree* continues in print and his collection of talks and essays, *The New Sentence* has gone through multiple printings. Since 1979, Silliman has been writing a poem entitled

The Alphabet. Volumes published thus far from that project have included *ABC, Demo to Ink, Jones, Lit, Manifest, N/O, Paradise, ®, Toner, What* and *Xing.* Salt will reissue his longpoem *Tjanting* in 2002.

RICK SMITH is a Clinical Psychologist who, with his wife, co-directs Back in the Saddle, a residential ranch for head-injured adults, in Apple Valley, California. He plays harmonica for the Hangan Brothers (*Mars Market,* 2000, Blue Cap Music). *The Wren Notebook* (2000, Lummox) is his most recent book. He and Erika are raising their 8 year-old son, Saunder.

ALAN SONDHEIM's books include the anthology *Being on Line: Net Subjectivity* (Lusitania, 1996), *Disorders of the Real* (Station Hill, 1988), and *.echo* (alt-X digital arts, 2001). His video and films have been shown internationally. Sondheim co-moderates several email lists, including Cybermind, Cyberculture, and Wryting and is currently Associate Editor of the online magazine Beehive. Sondheim teaches in the trAce online writing program, and this year is at Florida International University in Miami. Sondheim lives in Brooklyn; he lectures and publishes widely on contemporary art and Internet issues.

DENISE L. STEVENS' work has appeared in the *Alaska Quarterly Review.*

TERESE SVOBODA's fourth book of poetry, *Treason,* has just been published by Zoo Press.

PAULA SZUCHMAN is a poet and freelance journalist living in Brooklyn, New York. Her poetry has appeared in *Spork,* and her articles run regularly in *Travel & Leisure, The Daily Telegraph,* and *Time Out New York*

JAMES TATE is the author of numerous books of poetry, including *Memoir of the Hawk* (Ecco Press, 2001); *Shroud of the Gnome* (1997); and *Worshipful Company of Fletchers* (1994), which won the National Book Award.

JUDITH TAYLOR is the author of *Curios* (Sarabande Books, 2000), and *Burning* (Portlandia Press, 1999). Recent work has appeared in *Conduit, Fence,* and *Prairie Schooner* and the antholgies *Ravishing DisUnitites* (Wesleyan, 2000) and *Stand Up Poets* (Iowa, 2002). She is co-editor of *POOL: A Journal of Poetry.*

ELAINE TERRANOVA's latest book of poems is *The Dog's Heart* (Orchises Press, 2002). She has recent work appearing in *Prairie Schooner* and the *Midwest Quarterly.*

LESLIE ULLMAN is the author of three poetry collections, most recently *Slow Work Through Sand* published by University of Iowa Press. She directs the Creative Writing Program at University of Texas-El Paso and teaches in the Vermont College MFA Program.

CHARLES HARPER WEBB's latest collection of poems, *Tulip Farms and Liver Colonies*, was published in fall 2001 by BOA Editions. He teaches at California State University, Long Beach, and is a 2001-2002 Guggenheim fellow.

SUSAN WHEELER's books include *Bag 'O' Diamonds*, *Smokes*, and *Source Codes*. She teaches at Princeton University and the New School.

EVE WOOD is a writer and artist living in Los Angeles. Her poems have appeared in many journals, including *Best American Poetry 1997*, *The New Republic*, *TriQuarterly*, *The Seattle Review*, *Poetry*, and *The Antioch Review*. Her chapbook *Paper Frankenstein* was published by Beyond Baroque in 1998, and her book *Correspondences* was published in Europe in 1999.

RENATE WOOD has published two books, *Raised Underground* (Carnegie Mellon University Press, 1991) and *The Patience of Ice* (Northwestern University Press, 2000). She is on the faculty of the MFA Program for Writers at Warren Wilson College in Asheville, North Carolina and lives with her husband in Boulder, Colorado.

GAIL WRONSKY is the author of two books of poetry, *Dying for Beauty* and *Again the Gemini Are in the Orchard*. Her poems and critical essays have appeared in *Antioch Review*, *Denver Quarterly*, *Colorado Review*, *Boston Review*, *Virginia Quarterly Review* and other journals. She is the recipient of an Artists Fellowship from the California Arts Council. Her first novel, *The Love-talkers*, was recently published by Hollyridge Press.

"A beautifully written, brilliant, deeply philosophical novel."
— **Chuck Kinder**

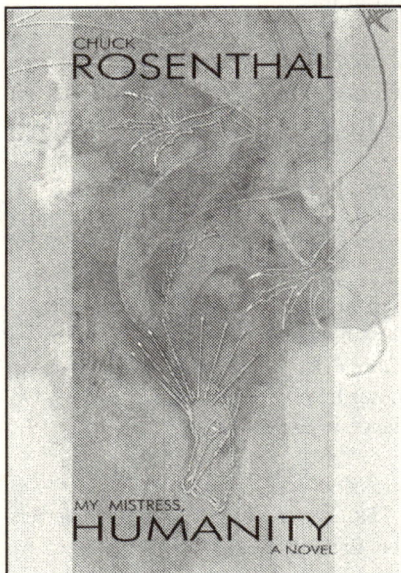

MY MISTRESS, HUMANITY

A Novel
by CHUCK ROSENTHAL

ISBN 0-9676003-5-9
$17.95 Softcover

Not far in the future a series of catastrophic weather events have crippled the technological infrastructure of the world and humankind is on the verge of total annihilation. One man knows the secret and only one young woman can save the planet. From Chuck Rosenthal comes an apocalyptic vision of the future, *My Mistress, Humanity*. Rosenthal's gothic vision of the future is both terrifying and beautiful. In the gorgeous lyric prose for which he's known, like the creator of a modern-day Frankenstein, Rosenthal takes us on a journey towards humanity's ultimate destruction and redemption.

Hollyridge Press

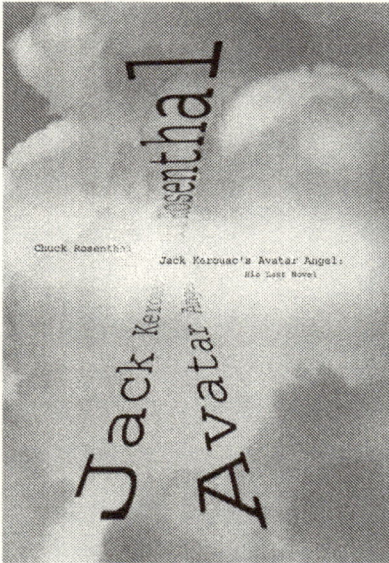

JACK KEROUAC'S AVATAR ANGEL

His Last Novel
by CHUCK ROSENTHAL

ISBN 0-9676003-2-4
$23.95 Hardcover

Chuck Rosenthal discovers a lost, unpublished manuscript from the King of the Beats—Jack Kerouac—who returns from the grave to set off one last time, charting chart the experience and conscience of a generation grappling with a changed culture. At once visionary and elegant, restless and incantatory, Rosenthal's writing achieves a rare beauty, his sensitivity to language as great as Kerouac's. In an exuberant novel of great wit and great loss, the emptiness Kerouac encounters in this final journey is palpable and tragic, unforeseen but inevitable, both familiar and foreign to America's most famous mystic traveler.

Hollyridge Press

"You will be dazzled and amazed."
— **David St. John**

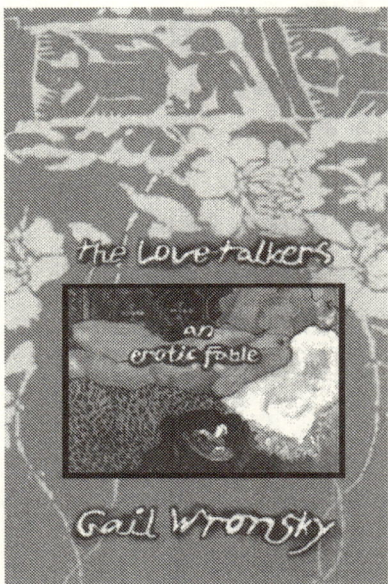

THE LOVE-TALKERS
An Erotic Fable
by GAIL WRONSKY

ISBN 0-9676003-3-2
$23.95 Hardcover

The beauty of Gail Wronsky's poetic language has never been better displayed than in *The Love-talkers*. Mexico City, with its parks and cathedrals provides a lush backdrop for the story. A sumptuously rendered book, celebrating passionate imagination with all the sublime joy of physical love, Wronsky's elegiac style summons up the magic of Latin American fiction in this novel of desire which brings us into the depths of erotic charge. From ecstatic awakenings to feverish enactments of appetite, Wronsky's novel reveals what happens when we find our deepest yearnings made true.

Hollyridge Press

"An amazing use of language and clarity of description compels the reader on."
—**Patricia Gulian**, *Book/Mark*

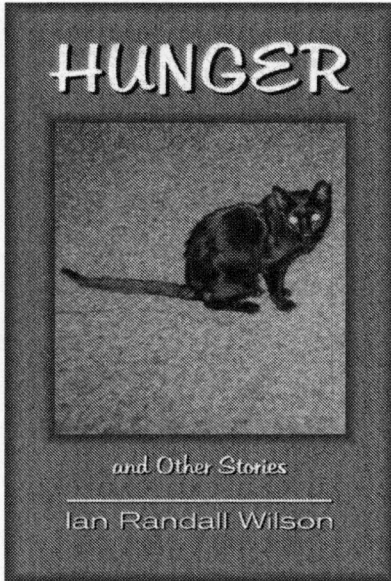

HUNGER
and Other Stories
by Ian Randall Wilson

ISBN 0-9676003-0-8
$12.95 Paperback

In his first collection of short stories, Ian Randall Wilson's characters are driven by intense yearnings for the satisfaction of their most basic human desires. All are thwarted by personal shortcomings, or the shortcomings of others, in their attempts to fulfill their longing. Here are 14 stories which "despite their restlessness," former *North American Review* editor Robley Wilson says, "glitter with persistent hopes."

Hollyridge Press

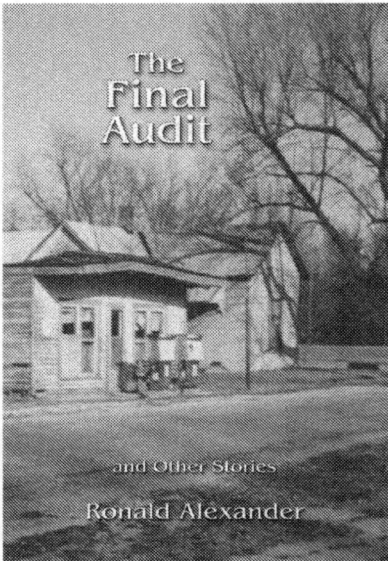

NEW POETRY ANNUAL
The best in American poetry!

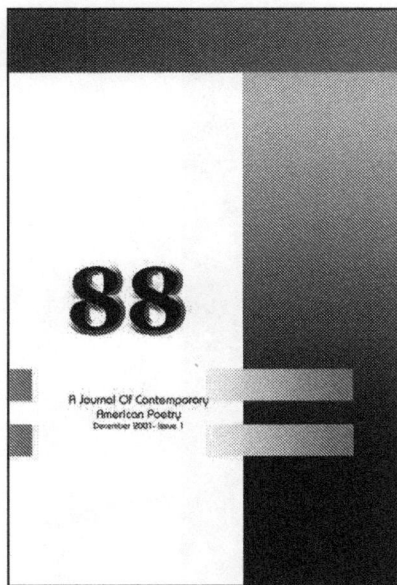

88

A Journal of Contemporary
American Poetry (Issue 1)

Denise L Stevens (editor)

ISBN 0-9676003-4-0
$13.95 Paperback

Issue 1 features an amazing range of poetry:

—The wonderfully comic sensibilities of Amiri Baraka: "I get horrible letters / From Ghosts / Demanding / Money."

—Dean Young writes in an echo of the New York School: "I don't ask for much: a little cleavage, / the honey of deconstruction to go along / with my cereal but something's scorched / my curtsey, one of my eyes's funny."

—Roger Weingarten's poignant narrative poem about fathers: "Into the no man's land / behind the flimsy curtain of my / resolve not to let them / get to me."

—Postmodernism from Gail Wronsky: "She's // greasy as a melancholy rhyme. What / self-esteems are   each day, paradoxically, / dismantled in her beehive?"

Plus essays and reviews. . .

Hollyridge Press

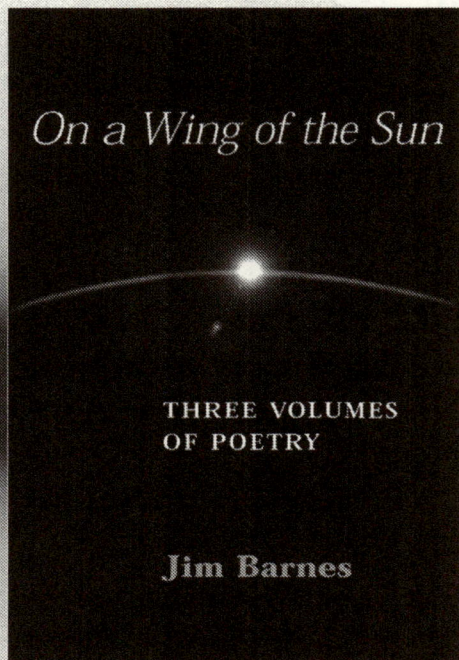

Guidelines

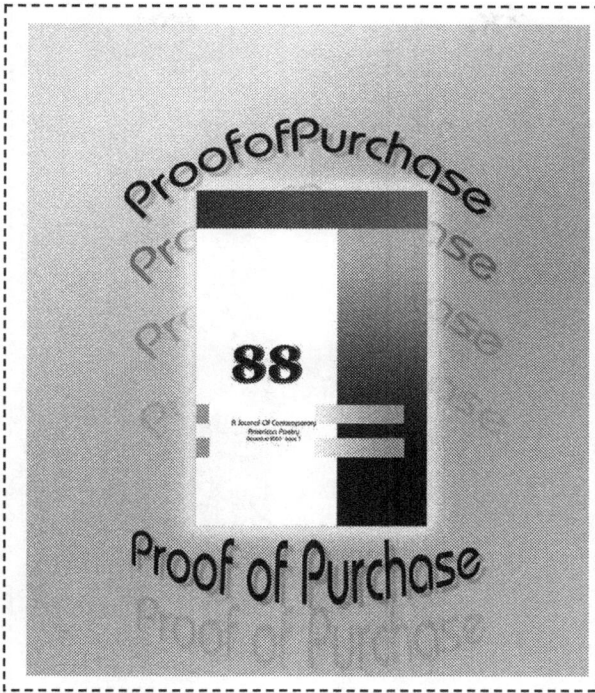

✂ cut along
dotted lines

Submission Guidelines

Unsolicited submissions will be considered March 1 through May 31 only. Unsolicited submissions postmarked outside that window will be returned unread. However, submissions accompanied by an original proof-of-purchase will be considered year round.

Manuscripts must be limited to five poems per submission with author name and address appearing on each page. Long poems not exceeding ten single spaced typewritten pages will be considered, but poems longer than three pages must be submitted separately.

Essays and reviews will also be considered. Please limit essays to no more than ten pages, double-spaced. Reviews must be no more than eight double-spaced pages.

At this time, material is being considered via USPS submission only. No disk, email or fax submissions. (However, if accepted, material must be provided later on disk.)

Include a self-addressed, stamped envelope for return of manuscripts. Submissions without SASE will be discarded unread. Cover letter with short bio, please. No simultaneous submissions or previously published material will be considered. We report on submissions within one to three months.

Mail submissions to: Editor, 88, c/o Hollyridge Press, P. O. Box 2872, Venice, CA 90294

Guidelines

ProofofPurchase

88

A Journal Of Contemporary
American Poetry

Proof of Purchase

Submission Guidelines

Unsolicited submissions will be considered March 1 through May 31 only. Unsolicited submissions postmarked outside that window will be returned unread. However, submissions accompanied by an original proof-of-purchase will be considered year round.

Manuscripts must be limited to five poems per submission with author name and address appearing on each page. Long poems not exceeding ten single spaced typewritten pages will be considered, but poems longer than three pages must be submitted separately.

Essays and reviews will also be considered. Please limit essays to no more than ten pages, double-spaced. Reviews must be no more than eight double-spaced pages.

At this time, material is being considered via USPS submission only. No disk, email or fax submissions. (However, if accepted, material must be provided later on disk.)

Include a self-addressed, stamped envelope for return of manuscripts. Submissions without SASE will be discarded unread. Cover letter with short bio, please. No simultaneous submissions or previously published material will be considered. We report on submissions within one to three months.

Mail submissions to: Editor, 88, c/o Hollyridge Press, P. O. Box 2872, Venice, CA 90294

www.ingramcontent.com/pod-product-compliance
Lightning Source LLC
LaVergne TN
LVHW011351080426
835511LV00005B/241